BLOOD SUGAR
THE FAMILY

NH
NEW
HOLLAND

MICHAEL MOORE

Inside

My Health, My Life

Welcome to my second *Blood Sugar* book: *The Family*. After my first *Blood Sugar* book, I met and talked with a wide cross-section of people about diabetes and living well. This motivated me to source new ingredients, modify my cooking techniques and learn more about healthy living for families. I have immersed myself even deeper into creating dishes that are delicious and surprisingly healthy.

Whatever the size and make up of your family, I have written this book to get you all thinking about the role that food plays in your life. Like many people, I simply have to look after myself and eat well to maintain my health. I achieve this by involving my family in all of my health and eating habits. I want to ensure my children understand the value of good healthy eating, as well as discovering the great joy that good food can play in their lives.

Many people have read about my story and the experiences that brought me to the point where I am today. For those of you who haven't, here's a quick recap!

From a very young age I could cook. It came to me naturally. I thrived on stress and achievement. So when it came to a career, I naturally chose one that was a 'pressure cooker'—a dynamic, growing industry where I could be creative. I chose to be a chef. I loved the daily challenge of a kitchen, the preparation and then the madness of service. Long hours, tough conditions and adversity—it was all part of the game and a large part of why I chose this industry. Going to work in the morning and putting on boots that were still soggy with sweat from the night before meant that I had worked hard; it was all part of the quest to push myself to the limit.

I still feel the same way and I often meet people in other professions who feel like me. They are nearly always in creative industries—art, music, food and design. I would love my kids to find this joy in their lives as they grow.

'Rise to the challenge and beat the odds, the competition is standing next to you.' This was my mantra, and I hoped it was going to help me fulfil my dreams.

When I was 35, I had just opened our new restaurant and my wife Angela had given birth to our first child, Eloise. I had been working night and day. I was feeling tired and run down, with an unusual thirst I just couldn't satisfy. I drank about 10 litres of lemon cordial in one night and ate a massive packet of jellybeans in one go. My body kept craving for more sugar as the days went on. I realised something was wrong and when my doctor tested me the next day, my blood sugar reading was 29 (normal is about 4). I was sent to the endocrinologist and officially diagnosed as diabetic. I may even have had diabetes my whole life.

My doctor said I was the most unusual person to become a diabetic. I was very fit, active and healthy; I never smoked nor was I a big drinker. I had always looked after myself, even while I worked long hours in an industry full of vices like alcohol, drugs and cigarettes. In fact, sometimes the only way to get a break during the day was to go for a 'smoke'—even if you didn't!

This came as a great shock.

I felt my life was in good order at that time. What could I possibly change to cope with this new diagnosis? For the first year or two it didn't seem so hard. I was just taking a couple of pills a day, increasing my exercise and laying off the sweet things. I was probably in denial, thinking it would just go away. Gradually my visits to the endocrinologist became further apart and less important. I was feeling fine and continued to pursue my very busy life.

I have since learnt this was a big mistake! Gradually my drug regime changed as the degeneration took effect and I became insulin dependent. I was still unaware of the serious health risks that diabetes carried.

Fast-forward ten years. One lazy Sunday I was out to dinner with my family. I remember it so clearly. It felt like I'd been hit by a truck. One minute I was standing at the barbecue, the next minute I hit the floor. My wife Angela was with me and at first she thought I was having a diabetic hypo. She called an ambulance immediately. When I wasn't able to drink lemonade to bring my sugars back up because my face was paralysed down one side, she realised it was more serious. She looked me in the eyes and said 'I think you've had a stroke, there's an ambulance coming'. My kids witnessed the whole thing and it took a while for Eloise, my daughter, to get the vision out of her head. It was very confronting for our family. Angela's quick thinking saved my life.

From this day, my life changed forever.

I was really scared for the first time in my life. I began to read and study what was going on. Some of the facts were really confronting. Why did this happen to me? There is no clear answer. There is a link to diabetes, but in my case there is still no firm conclusion as to why I had the stroke. I was told the chances of another stroke occurring within days after the initial one were quite high.

I lay in hospital hoping that my body would not suffer another stroke. It was like waiting for the ball to drop into place on the roulette wheel; it seemed to spin forever. If someone had said to me at this point, 'Give me everything you own and I'll guarantee that you can walk along the beach at the weekend with your wife and kids', I'd have taken the deal. Luckily I did manage to walk along the beach with my family on the day I was discharged from hospital. It was the best day of my life!

In the weeks before the stroke I felt super fit—riding my bike, running, going to the gym. I just remember feeling great and strong. However, while at the gym a week before it happened, the floor did go soft and feel spongy under my feet and my legs gave way. I didn't fall over but it was a strange feeling. Maybe this was a small warning, but who knows? If you have experienced anything like this, go to your doctor—I wish I had.

The stroke was caused by a large blood clot that ran up my neck, through the clear veins of a fit young man. It fired into my brain and fortunately landed in a place where it did not cause too much damage.

Obviously I had to rethink all of the food that I had been eating to manage diabetes and keep my health on track, but was determined to continue eating quality food, so decided to write the first *Blood Sugar* book, to provide some light into the 'gastronomic wilderness' of diet food. In September 2012, I launched my restaurant in Sydney, O Bar and Dining, where I have created a menu that is underpinned by the *Blood Sugar* healthy eating philosophy.

There is no cure, yet, for diabetes. In the meantime, I respect it and realize it is always with me but do not become a victim or a sufferer. Recently I have been involved in the launch of the iBGStar Blood Glucose Meter that connects to your iPhone or iPod. It's a fantastic device that can connect you directly to your doctor and I believe it is going to be a game changer.

One of the benefits of writing books and being prepared to speak publicly about diabetes and stroke is that I have come into contact with many health professionals who are looking at and researching blood pressure, cholesterol and diabetes. They all have my ongoing support and appreciation. The result of all those conversations is this second book. I have not written a diet book—it is a lifestyle book, a collection of recipes my family and I love to eat that help to keep us on track.

I hope this book gives you some inspiration to get yourself, your friends and family around the table.

Michael Moore

The Carbohydrate Exchange

You will notice that most of the recipes in this book have a number next to them. This is the recipe's carbohydrate exchange number, calculated from all its ingredients.

It is only really relevant to diabetics, especially people with type 1 or insulin dependant type 2.

These people need to be aware of the carbohydrate exchange number in a meal or a dish in order for them to work out the correct amount of insulin to administer.

They will need to work out how their own bodies process the carbohydrate and balance that with the correct amount of insulin. This should be done with their doctor. This can be a tiresome, but necessary, process for insulin dependant diabetics.

I am very happy that my recipes all have a low exchange number. I really hope that by including this information it helps them enjoy the food in this book with confidence

We have calculated:

ONE CARBOHYDRATE EXCHANGE EQUALS
15 grams or ½ oz of carbohydrate

This is sometimes called one carbohydrate choice.

Breakfast

chilled apple, pear & quinoa porridge with raw almonds

SERVES 4

12 fl oz (355ml) skim milk

4 fl oz (120ml) water

4oz (120g) white quinoa

4oz (120g) plain yoghurt

1 tablespoon agave nectar

1 red apple

1 green pear

pinch ground ginger

pinch ground cinnamon

2oz (60g) raw almonds, skin on, finely sliced

1. Place milk, water and quinoa in a small saucepan, bring to the boil, and reduce to a simmer and cover. Cook, stirring occasionally, for approximately 15 minutes until soft, then allow to cool.

2. Place cooked quinoa in a mixing bowl and stir in the yoghurt and agave nectar. Using a coarse cheese grater, grate the apple and pear into the bowl, including any of the juice.

3. Mix together well. Add the spices to taste and adjust consistency with a splash of milk.

4. Place into small serving bowls and sprinkle with the chopped almonds.

Tip: Quinoa is a highly nutritious South American seed that can be substituted for most grains. It's available from health food stores and supermarkets.

One of my favorite breakfast dishes. A little goes a long way. Feel free to add seasonal berries or fruit of your choice.

Rainy day hot milk & barley porridge

SERVES 4

16 fl oz (475ml) milk (2% fat)

2 tablespoons agave nectar

1 cinnamon quill

1 vanilla bean or teaspoon of vanilla
  essence

1 tablespoon sultanas

3oz (80g) rolled barley flakes

2 tablespoons sunflower seeds

2 tablespoons pumpkin seeds

2 tablespoons flaked almonds

pinch ground nutmeg

1. In a medium-sized saucepan, heat 12 fl oz (350ml) of milk with the agave nectar, cinnamon quill and the split vanilla bean or essence. Stir in the sultanas and the barley flakes and cook over a low heat for 10 minutes, stirring until thick and the barley is soft.

2. Meanwhile, in a preheated, non-stick frying pan cook together the sunflower, pumpkin seeds and flaked almonds until toasted and light brown. Allow to cool, then add to the porridge.

3. To serve, bring the remaining milk to the boil, whisking to make as much froth as possible (I use my coffee machine steamer to do this). Spoon the porridge into serving bowls, spoon some of the hot milk froth on top and dust with the ground nutmeg.

This is a lower Gi version of traditional oat porridge, and is perfect for winter mornings. You'll find flaked barley in supermarkets and at food markets.

crunchy nut, seed & oat clusters

MAKES APPROXIMATELY 40 SMALL CLUSTERS, SERVES 8 (5 PER PORTION)

4oz (120g) barley oat flakes

3oz (80g) nibbed almonds

2oz (60g) flax seeds

3oz (80g) unsalted peanuts chopped

2oz (60g) hazelnuts chopped

2oz (60g) pumpkin seeds

2oz (60g) sunflower seeds

2oz (60g) dried apricots, chopped

2oz (60g) cornflour

3oz (80g) agave nectar

1 teaspoon vanilla essence

3oz (80g) butter

3 large egg whites

1 tablespoon caster (superfine) sugar

fresh figs, natural yoghurt and milk,
    to serve

1. Preheat oven to 360°F/180°C. In a large mixing bowl combine all dry ingredients and mix well.

2. In a small saucepan melt together the agave nectar, vanilla essence and the butter. Pour over the dry ingredients and stir thoroughly, coating the dry ingredients as much as possible.

2. Using a whisk, vigorously beat the egg whites to a firm peak, adding the caster sugar at the end. Add the dry ingredients to the egg whites and mix well.

3. Place a sheet of baking parchment onto a baking tray, lightly spray with oil and place teaspoon-sized drops of the mixture at regular intervals, being careful not to let clusters touch each other.

4. Place in the oven and cook for 10 minutes, then reduce temperature to 300°F/150°C and cook for a further 20 minutes. Remove clusters from the oven and allow to cool. The clusters should be lightly coloured, dry and crunchy.

5. Store in a sealed container for up to 3 weeks. Serve with fresh figs, natural yoghurt and milk.

This is my alternative to highly-sugared commercial cereals. My kids love them and can't tell the difference.

Greek yoghurt parfait cups

SERVES 4

1 tablespoon unprocessed bran

10oz (300g) natural low-fat Greek
    yoghurt

1 tablespoon quinoa flakes

3 fl oz (100ml) grape juice or apple
    juice

1 cup of water

1 red apple

1 tablespoon agave nectar

½ punnet fresh blueberries

½ punnet fresh raspberries

1. In a small bowl mix the bran, yoghurt, quinoa flakes and grape juice, then place in the fridge.

2. In a small saucepan heat the agave nectar with water. Peel and deseed the apple then cut it into 8 wedges. Poach these apples over a simmering heat for 10 minutes until soft and tender. Add the blueberries and raspberries, remove from the heat and allow fruit to cool in the liquid.

3. Remove fruit from the saucepan using a slotted spoon and layer alternately with the yoghurt mixture into serving glasses. Place in the fridge to cool before serving.

Tip: Quinoa is a highly nutritious South American seed that can be substituted for most grains. It's available from health food stores and supermarkets.

POaChEd rEd fruit Salad

SERVES 4

6 fl oz (180ml) water

2oz (60g) agave nectar

1 small piece of fresh ginger, grated

1 small bunch rhubarb

1 punnet of strawberries

4 fresh black figs

2oz (60g) organic red or white quinoa

12 fl oz (350ml) water

½ bunch fresh mint

1. Preheat oven to 360°F/180°C. In a small saucepan heat water and dissolve the agave nectar. Add grated ginger. Using a vegetable peeler, peel the rhubarb and cut into 1inch (3cm) batons. Place the rhubarb into saucepan with agave liquid and cook on a low heat for approximately 2 minutes.

2. Trim the stalks from the strawberries. Cut the figs and strawberries in half and place them into an ovenproof dish. Pour the hot poached rhubarb and liquid over them. Place dish into oven for 5 minutes, remove and allow to cool in the liquid.

3. Place the quinoa in a small saucepan and cover with water. Bring to the boil and simmer for 15 minutes until plumped and tender, then drain and rinse under cold water.

4. Drain the liquid from the fruit and add it to the cooked quinoa with the finely chopped mint leaves.

5. Arrange the fruit on serving dishes and spoon the sweetened quinoa on the top.

Tip: Quinoa is a highly nutritious South American seed that can be substituted for most grains. It's available from health food stores and supermarkets.

soft & chewy breakfast bars

MAKES 12 BARS

4oz (120g) barley oat flakes

2 wheat breakfast cereal biscuits such
   as Vitabrits or Weet Bix.

2oz (60g) pumpkin seeds

2oz (60g) pistachio nuts, chopped

2oz (60g) sunflower seeds

1oz (30g) white sesame seeds

1oz (30g) millet

1oz (30g)flax seeds

1oz (30g) chia seeds

2oz (60g) dried cranberries, chopped

pinch dried ginger

pinch ground cinnamon

3oz (80g) butter

3oz (80g) agave nectar

3oz (80g) honey

1. Preheat oven to 360°F/180°C degrees. In a large mixing bowl combine all dry ingredients, mix well.

2. In a small saucepan melt the butter, agave nectar and the honey. Pour this over the dry ingredients and stir, thoroughly coating the dry ingredients.

3. Line a baking tray with baking parchment and spray it lightly with oil. Pour mixture in and lightly flatten using the palm of your hand.

4. Place tray in oven and bake for 25 minutes, remove and allow to cool for 2 minutes in the tray. Using a large kitchen knife mark cut lines approximately 3 x 1inches (18 x 3 cm) wide. Place in refrigerator until set.

5. Once set, break or cut bars into pieces and store in an airtight container for up to 3 weeks.

Tip: Chia seeds, known as the Aztec 'super food' are one of the highest plant sources of Omega 3 fatty acids, as well as being rich in vitamins and fibre.

My kids love these bars – they don't take them to school because of the nuts, but they are easy to make for a weekend or after-school treat.

Homemade ricotta

MAKES 12 SERVES

2 pints (1.2 litres) full cream milk
1 pint (600ml) buttermilk
1 pint (600ml) light cream
large pinch of sea salt
1 lemon, juiced

1. Place a large strainer over a large mixing bowl and cover it with a piece of fine muslin or cheesecloth.

2. In a large heavy-based saucepan mix the milk, buttermilk and cream together. Place on a medium heat and, continually stirring, gradually bring up to a slow rolling boil, or 345°F/175°C.

3. Add a pinch of salt and stir in the lemon juice. Continue to stir until the curds and whey separate. This occurs quickly, so as soon as this happens remove pan from heat and gently stir for a minute.

4. Carefully pour all of the contents into the strainer and allow to drain until all the liquid (whey) has collected in the bowl. The curds (cheese) should be firm to touch. Place in a separate bowl in the fridge to cool. Keeps in the fridge for 5 days.

Tip: Reserve whey liquid to use in making bread or pizza bases, it can also be reused to make a sharper ricotta by adding more milk and rennet.

This ricotta is so easy to make and is the basis for many of my favorite recipes. A purist will say that this is not 'real ricotta' because it is not made from the whey. But for me it is far superior to the off-the-shelf products available and a very useful ingredient.

FluFFy lemon ricotta hotcakes

MAKES 8 HOTCAKES

2 large eggs

2oz (60g) stoneground flour

2oz (60g) self-raising (bakers) flour

1½ cups skimmed milk

½ teaspoon bicarbonate of soda

1 cup fresh ricotta cheese (see
　　Homemade Ricotta in this section)

juice and zest of one lemon

2 tablespoons agave nectar

2 tablespoons ground almonds

2 tablespoons flax seeds/linseeds

2 egg whites

icing sugar for dusting

1. In a small bowl whisk together whole eggs, flour, milk and bicarbonate of soda to form a batter the consistency of thick cream. In a separate bowl, whisk the egg whites to firm peaks and fold this into the batter.

2. In another small bowl, stir the ricotta, lemon zest and agave nectar together with the ground almonds and flax seeds.

3. Heat a medium-sized non-stick frying pan, spray with a little oil and add a large spoon of the batter to form a hotcake about 4 inches (10cm) across. Working quickly, add a tablespoon of the seed and ricotta mix to the hotcake.

4. Allow each hotcake to form bubbles on the surface and cook for 2 minutes then flip over and cook for another 2 minutes.

5. Serve hotcakes with a light dusting of icing sugar and a squeeze of fresh lemon.

Tip: Flax seeds are high in nutrients and Omega 3 and help lower the Gi of the dish.

soft boiled egg dippers with potato hash & salt beef

SERVES 4

6oz (175g) piece brined beef silverside
   or brisket

¼ of a small white cabbage,
   finely shredded

sea salt and pepper

1 tablespoon white vinegar

½ medium onion

½ medium potato (Nicola)

½ medium sweet potato

1 fl oz (30ml) vegetable oil

8 large eggs at room temperature

wholewheat toast to serve (not
   included in carb exchange)

1. Cook the silverside in a pot of lightly salted simmering water until tender for approximately 1 hour. Test by piercing with a small skewer. It should slide through the meat with no resistance. Remove from heat and allow beef to cool in the liquid. Once cool, use a fork to shred finely.

2. Meanwhile, cook the cabbage in a small pan just covered with cold water, a pinch of salt and the white vinegar. Bring to the boil and simmer until tender. Drain in a colander and set aside.

3. Using a coarse cheese grater shred the onion and potatoes into a bowl. Heat a medium-sized non-stick frying pan, add the vegetable oil and fry the potato and onion mixture for 10 minutes stirring frequently. Once the potato is tender add the drained cabbage and finely shredded salt beef. Continue to cook for a further 5 minutes.

4. Meanwhile, place eggs into a small pot of cold water and bring to the boil. Simmer for 4 minutes for runny eggs and 5 minutes for medium. Remove from the heat and place into egg cups for serving.

5. Cut the tops off the eggs and spoon as much of the cooked hash as you can onto each of them.

32

This is a great protein boost, especially for kids. The dish is also good with shaved ham or turkey.

Egg, bacon & mushroom pita pockets

SERVES 4

1 teaspoon olive oil

2 rashers of bacon shredded

1 medium sized onion, finely chopped

6oz (175g) button mushrooms, sliced

8 large organic eggs

2 tablespoons light cream

sea salt and pepper

1 small knob of butter

4 small wholewheat pita bread pockets
    or soft tacos

1. Heat a small non-stick frying pan, add olive oil and fry bacon with the onion for a few minutes. Add the sliced mushrooms and cook for 5 minutes until any liquid has evaporated. Cover and keep warm.

2. Crack the eggs into a small bowl, add the cream, sea salt and pepper and lightly whisk with a fork.

3. In another small non-stick frying pan add a small knob of butter, and as it begins to sizzle pour in the eggs and cook over a medium heat, stirring with a wooden spoon or spatula. Allow the eggs to settle in the pan and stir gently so they are creamy and scrambled.

4. Place the pita pockets in a medium oven 360°F/180°C for approximately 3 minutes. Slice the top off each pita pocket and open them. Spoon in the scrambled egg mix and place the bacon and mushrooms on the top. If using soft tacos, warm them on a griddle pan first, fill with the scrambled eggs and bacon, then fold and serve.

chickpea & corn fritters with bacon & avocado

MAKES 8 FRITTERS (2 PER PORTION)

1 medium brown onion

sea salt and pepper

4 rashers of bacon

4oz (120g) fresh ricotta

3 eggs

6 fl oz (175ml) milk (2% fat)

4oz (120g) stone ground wholemeal
  flour

½ teaspoon bicarbonate of soda

10oz (300g) chickpeas, cooked washed
  and drained

6oz (175g) canned sweet corn kernels
  drained

1 ripe avocado

½ lemon

1 tablespoon sumac (middle eastern)
  spice

1 fl oz (30ml) vegetable oil

1. Preheat oven to 360°F/180°C. Peel the onion and cut into 8 wedges, drizzle with a little oil then season with sea salt and pepper. Cook in the oven for 20 minutes until soft and golden. Remove from oven and sprinkle with sumac spices. Keep warm.

2. Grill the bacon in a hot pan or on a barbecue plate until crispy.

3. In a small bowl mix the ricotta with a small whisk until smooth. Add the eggs and milk and whisk together briskly. Gradually add the flour and bicarbonate of soda to form a batter; it should be quite thick.

4. Roughly chop half of the chickpeas and mix both the chopped and whole chickpeas into the batter. Add the corn to the batter and season with a pinch of salt and pepper.

5. In another bowl mash the avocado with the back of a fork until broken down, season with sea salt and pepper and juice of half a lemon.

6. Heat a small non-stick frying pan, spray with a little oil and spoon in the batter. Add small fritters, approximately 3 inches (8cm) in diameter, and cook over a medium heat for 3-4 minutes each side.

7. Serve on a warm plate with the avocado, the roasted onions and the hot rashers of bacon.

This is a filling and nourishing breakfast. I often cook fritters in advance and pop them into the kids' lunch box.

Protein boost, scrambled eggs with tomatoes

SERVES 4

8 ripe Roma tomatoes

sea salt and pepper

1 clove fresh garlic, crushed

1 medium red chili, finely chopped

½ teaspoon caster (superfine) sugar

8 large eggs

4 egg whites

3oz (80g) silken tofu

2 tablespoons olive oil

½ bunch fresh basil

Grainy bread, toasted, to serve

1. Preheat oven to 300°F/180°C. Halve the tomatoes lengthways and place onto a baking tray. Brush with half the olive oil, then season with sea salt and pepper.

2. Spread tomatoes with the crushed garlic and chopped chili, then dust lightly with caster sugar.

3. Place onto a tray and roast in oven for 25-35 minutes.

4. Meanwhile, in a mixing bowl place the whole eggs, egg whites and tofu; whisk well together and season with sea salt and pepper.

5. Heat a medium-sized non-stick frying pan over a high heat, add the remaining olive oil. Add the fresh basil leaves and cook for 10 seconds. Add the eggs and tofu mixture, leave to cook for 10 seconds without stirring and, using chopsticks or a wooden spoon, gradually stir the eggs from the outside of the pan to the centre.

6. Once eggs and tofu become creamy, remove from the heat. The scrambled eggs should be undercooked and slightly liquid, however, the eggs will continue to cook in the pan. Serve on grainy toasted bread with the roasted tomatoes.

Hot smoked salmon & sweet potato omelette

SERVES 4

2 medium-sized sweet potatoes

sea salt and pepper

2oz (60g) butter

½ bunch continental parsley, chopped

juice of ½ lemon, plus extra to serve

10oz (300g) hot smoked salmon or
    ocean trout

6 large eggs

6 egg whites

1 fl oz (30ml) olive oil

optional sourdough or wholegrain
    bread, toasted, (not included in
    carb exchange)

1. Wash and peel the sweet potato and, using a coarse cheese grater, grate into a bowl. Season with a little salt and pepper.

2. Heat a medium-sized non-stick pan, melt the butter and add the sweet potato. Cook slowly over a medium heat for 10 minutes until soft and cooked through. Stir in the chopped parsley and a squeeze of the lemon juice.

3. Pick through the smoked salmon to remove any skin or small bones. Using your fingers, flake salmon into a bowl. Set aside.

4. In a separate bowl, mix the whole eggs and egg whites thoroughly, add a pinch of sea salt and some fresh ground pepper.

5. Heat a small non-stick frying pan and spray or wipe with a small amount of olive oil on a paper towel. Add a ladle of the egg mix to the pan and cook to form each omelette. Add some of the hot sweet potato mixture to the centre of the omelette and flake some of the salmon on the top.

6. Using the back of a fork flip half over and roll into a tube. Place each omelette onto a serving plate and serve with lemon wedges or slices and toasted grainy or sourdough bread.

This is full of flavor and goodness, and being low Gi, it will fill you up. For me it's a win all round!

Roasted field mushrooms with crumbled feta & garlic

SERVES 4

8 large field mushroom caps
1 clove of fresh garlic
2oz (60g) butter
4oz (120g) low-fat feta cheese
½ bunch lemon thyme
1 cup of fresh baby spinach leaves
4 slices of soy linseed bread, toasted,
   optional
sea salt and pepper

1. Preheat oven to 360°F/180°C. Peel and remove stalks from the mushrooms. Heat a non-stick frying pan and cook mushrooms together with sliced garlic and butter for approximately 5 minutes.

2. Turn mushrooms onto a roasting tray and sprinkle with lemon thyme and crumbled feta. Bake in oven for 12 minutes, until cooked and tender and the cheese begins to melt.

3. Toast the bread and spread with a little butter. Place some of the spinach leaves on each slice and spoon on the hot mushrooms and cheese. Serve in the middle of the table, to share.

44

I like to add some rashers of grilled bacon, shaved ham or poached eggs.

Baked Chili eggs With Chickpeas, spinach & shaved ham

SERVES 4

2 tablespoons olive oil

1 medium onion, finely diced

1 clove garlic

pinch smoked paprika

½ teaspoon dried chili flakes

4 ripe tomatoes, chopped

1 x 10oz (300g) can of organic
   chickpeas

sea salt and pepper

2 cups fresh spinach leaves

8 large eggs

6oz (175g) finely shaved smoked ham

grainy bread, toasted, optional
   to serve (not included in carb
   exchange)

1. Preheat oven to 360°F/180°C. In a medium-sized non-stick frying pan heat one tablespoon of the olive oil and fry together the onion and garlic until light brown. Add a pinch of the paprika, chili flakes and the chopped tomatoes. Cook on a low heat for 15 minutes until a rich sauce has formed.

2. Add the chickpeas and cook a further 20 minutes. Season with sea salt and fresh pepper, and add more chili to taste.

3. In 4 small ovenproof dishes or ramekins, divide the spinach leaves and spoon over the hot tomato chickpea mix. Using the back of a serving spoon make a well on the top. Crack two eggs into each well. If you like your eggs really spicy, sprinkle some chili flakes or fresh chili on the eggs at this point.

4. Drizzle the top with a few drops of olive oil and bake for approximately 12 minutes until the eggs are cooked to your liking. Place shaved ham on the top and serve with some hot grainy bread, toasted.

The paprika and chili will stimulate your metabolism and get your body moving — it's a perfect spicy kickstart to your day.

strawberry mojito, basil, lime & ginger

SERVES 4

½ punnet of large ripe strawberries

2 fresh limes cut into wedges

1 small knob of fresh ginger finely grated

4 teaspoons agave nectar

1 pint (600ml) of ice

1 pint (600ml) sparkling mineral or soda water or diet lemonade

8 leaves of fresh green basil

8 leaves of fresh garden mint

1. Trim stalks from the strawberries and cut into quarters. Divide the limes, grated ginger and strawberries equally between your 4 large glasses. Add a teaspoon of agave nectar and one basil and mint leaf to each glass.

2. Using a muddling stick, or the handle of a wooden spoon crush ingredients together for a minute or two until combined and fragrant.

3. Fill the 4 glasses with ice, top up with the sparkling mineral water and stir using a long cocktail spoon.

Tip: Swap with different berries when they are in season.

High Protein iced espresso coffee ripple

SERVES 4

2oz (60g) whey protein powder
(vanilla flavor)

2 pints almond milk

3oz (80g) silken tofu

2 egg whites

2 tablespoons agave nectar

4 shots of black espresso coffee

½ teaspoon ground cinnamon

4 large cups of ice

1. In a large jug place the protein powder, almond milk, tofu and egg white with the agave nectar. Using a stick blender combine well together for 1 minute until very smooth.

2. Fill serving glasses with ice. Pour the milk mixture over the ice to almost fill the glass.

3. Make espresso or fresh pressed coffee and allow it to cool slightly, then pour over the top and serve immediately.

get up & go mango

SERVES 4

8 fresh raspberries

2 tablespoons agave nectar

1 large fresh ripe mango

1 small ripe banana

8oz (240g) natural plain yoghurt

4oz (120g) silken tofu

1 pint (600ml) low-fat milk

3½ fl oz (100ml) fresh orange juice

1 cup of ice

1. Place raspberries and one tablespoon of agave nectar into a small bowl and mash with a fork until broken down. Set aside until serving.

2. Cut mango in half and remove flesh and skin from both halves. Place the mango with remaining ingredients into a blender and blend for 1 minute until smooth and thick.

3. Place a spoon of the fresh raspberry mixture into each glass and pour the mango liquid on top.

A perfect early morning treat before a good walk.

spiced virgin Mary with oyster, celery & jalapeno

SERVES 4

pinch of fennel seeds

pinch of cilantro/coriander seeds

pinch of black peppercorns

500g (1lb) fresh ripe tomatoes (diced)

½ clove of fresh garlic, grated

1 small piece jalapeno chili

2 fl oz (60ml) red wine vinegar

1 teaspoon agave nectar

pinch sea salt

1 cup of ice

4 freshly opened oysters

1 large stalk celery, cut into sticks

1. Heat the spices and pepper in a small frying pan for a few minutes until they are fragrant, transfer to a mortar and pestle and grind to a powder.

2. In a bowl place the diced tomato with the grated garlic, chopped jalapeno and the spice powder. Add the red wine vinegar, agave nectar and a pinch of sea salt cover with plastic wrap and leave in fridge for minimum 3 hours or overnight.

3. Pour tomato mixture into a blender or use a stick blender to puree to a juice and strain through a fine strainer into a jug with some ice.

4. Place one oyster in the bottom of a shot glass garnish with a small stick of celery. Adjust the seasoning of the juice to your taste, top each glass with the juice and serve cold.

Dark chocolate, nut & banana thick shake

SERVES 4

2oz (60g) dark chocolate

1 teaspoon of agave nectar

1 tablespoon cocoa (unsweetened)

1 pint (600ml) almond milk

1 large ripe banana

1 tablespoon honey

4 fl oz (120ml) natural yoghurt

4 fl oz (120ml) silken tofu

2 tablespoons ground almonds

2 tablespoons whey protein powder
   (vanilla or chocolate)

1 cup of ice

1. In a small glass bowl melt the chocolate and agave in the microwave for approximately 20 seconds, then set aside.

2. Combine the cocoa with a little of the milk to make a paste then mix it with all the remaining ingredients. Place mixture into a blender or a large jug and, using a stick blender, blend until smooth.

3. Spoon a little melted chocolate into your serving glasses. Use the back of a spoon to spread around the inside of the glass.

4. Pour the thick shake over and serve with a little grated chocolate.

Yum, this is a delicious treat to start the day. Drink it with a high protein low carb breakfast such as an omelette.

Fresh Vegetable Juice

SERVES 4

4 celery stalks

2 large carrots

2 green apples

2 medium sized beetroot

1oz (30g) fresh ginger

GARNISH

1 orange peeled and sliced

½ small cucumber thinly sliced

4 large strawberries

2 cups of ice

4 sprigs of fresh mint

1. Prepare your glasses by placing some of the sliced orange, cucumber and fresh strawberries with the ice in the bottom of the glasses.

2. Wash all vegetables well. Just before serving, pass all vegetables and fruit through a juicer, pour into a jug and stir together.

3. Pour the juice into the prepared glasses and serve with a sprig of mint.

Snacks & Sandwiches

pack 'n' go snack bags

ADAPT THE INGREDIENTS FOR ONE, TWO OR A GROUP OF KIDS.

GIANT TRAIL MIX

pepitas

raw cashew nuts

raw peanuts

dried apples

dried apricots

dried prunes

whole almonds

CRISPY SALAD BAGS

celery sticks

baby cherry tomatoes

baby corn cobs

sliced red peppers

carrot sticks

green beans

TROPICAL FRUIT TREATS

sliced fresh pineapple

sliced fresh mango

black figs

red cherries

BERRY BAGS

strawberries

blueberries

raspberries

GIANT TRAIL MIX

1. Roast the pepitas, cashew nuts and peanuts in a 360°F/180°C oven for 12 minutes, and allow to cool before placing in the bags. Mix your preferred selection of remaining ingredients, making sure to include plenty of seeds and nuts.

CRISPY SALAD BAGS

1. Peel celery stick with a potato peeler to remove the string, and peel carrots before making them into sticks. Wash and drain all remaining ingredients. Cut in large pieces to retain freshness, mix to create bright and healthy snacks.

TROPICAL FRUIT TREATS

1. Wash and dry the figs, cut the mango cheeks, leaving the skin on and slice a criss-cross into the flesh with a small knife. When they are ready to eat, invert the slices to eat each small square at a time. Leave the stones in the cherries and also leave the skin on the pineapple slices, it will keep fresh.

BERRY BAGS

1. Wash and dry all the berries, handling them carefully as they are fragile. Change the berries to whatever is in season, and keep as chilled as possible. Berries are high in fibre but also sugar, so keep portion sizes small.

These are easy and quick to prepare. Involve your kids in packing them—why not seal the bags with coloured clothes pegs for some fun? Feel free to be creative.

Thick & spicy-sweet sunflower butter

MAKES 1 LARGE JAR, OR APPROXIMATELY 24 SERVES

10oz (300g) sunflower seeds
1 tablespoon light olive oil
pinch ground ginger
pinch ground cinnamon
½ teaspoon vanilla bean paste
1 tablespoon agave nectar

1. Preheat oven to 360°F/180°C. Place sunflower seeds on a small baking tray lined with baking parchment and place in oven for 6-8 minutes until toasty but not dark brown. Remove seeds from the oven and allow to cool.

2. Once at room temperature place the sunflower seeds into a blender or food processor and chop to a fine crumb. This will take approximately 5 -10 minutes depending on the power of your blender. Add remaining ingredients to sunflower crumb and continue to blend until a smooth paste is formed. This may take a while. Adjust sweetness and spices to your own taste.

3. Remove and store in a clean tightly sealed jar.

This paste is a healthy nut-free alternative to peanut butter.

Quick roll-ups

MAKES 8 ROLL-UPS

4 soft taco or mountain bread wraps

1 avocado

4oz (120g) shaved chicken, ham or
canned tuna

8 slices of low-fat cheese or cream
cheese if serving cold

1 punnet grape tomatoes

1. To serve warm, lay bread onto a clean baking tray, spread with a little cream cheese or place a slice of cheese on each one. Layer other ingredients over cheese, and place into a medium-hot oven for 10 minutes to heat through.

2. Remove from oven and while still warm, roll up like a wrap, securing with a twist of baking parchment.

3. To serve cold, spread bread with cream cheese and layer other ingredients as you prefer. Lay onto a small sheet of greaseproof paper and roll as a wrap.

TWO-bite Chili beef Sliders

MAKES 4 SLIDERS

BEEF PATTIES

8oz (240g) lean beef mince

1 whole egg

pinch onion powder

sea salt and pepper

2 tablespoons sourdough
    breadcrumbs

½ teaspoon Worcestershire Sauce

½ teaspoon English mustard

½ teaspoon grated horseradish

2 tablespoons of pickled sweet chilies
    (see Basics section)

2 tablespoons low-fat mayonnaise (see
    Basics section)

4 small cob lettuce leaves

4 small seeded burger or
    brioche buns

1. Place all beef patty ingredients together in a small bowl and combine.

2. Divide into four equal parts and shape into small burger patties using a pallete knife. Put between 2 small sheets of greaseproof paper and refrigerate until required.

3. On a hot barbecue plate or in a non-stick frying pan cook the burger patties for 2 minutes each side until done to your liking.

4. Slice the burger buns in half and toast them lightly. Spread the bottom half with the low-fat mayo. Add a small lettuce leaf to each one, then the burger patties, and spoon over some of the pickled sweet chilies. Insert a small bamboo skewer through the middle of each slider and serve immediately.

Everyone loves a slider or mini burger. The chilies are spicy but not too hot.

shrimp & cucumber sliders

MAKES 4 SLIDERS

½ small Lebanese cucumber

sea salt and pepper

1 teaspoon olive oil

juice of ½ lemon

1 tablespoon natural yoghurt

½ bunch of fresh fennel tips

4 small seeded burger or
    brioche buns

8 large cooked shrimps (prawns)
    peeled and sliced

1. Using a mandolin slicer, thinly shred the cucumber into a small bowl. Season cucumber with sea salt and pepper, add the olive oil and a squeeze of lemon juice, leave to stand for 10 minutes to soften.

2. Stir together the yoghurt and the picked fennel tips.

3. Drain any liquid from the cucumber and stir in the yoghurt to coat it. Season with freshly ground pepper.

4. Slice open the dinner rolls and layer the cucumbers and sliced prawns alternately on the buns. Pierce the centre of each roll with a small bamboo skewer and serve.

Light and fresh, these tasty little shrimp rolls are great fun for entertaining.

seared spice-crusted tuna slider

MAKES 4 SLIDERS

pinch black sesame seeds

pinch white sesame seeds

½ teaspoon Sansho or Szechuan
   pepper

pinch ground ginger

pinch sweet paprika

sea salt and pepper

2oz (60g) Chinese cabbage
   (wombok), finely shredded

½ lemon juiced

1 teaspoon soy sauce

4oz (120g) fresh tuna fillet

½ teaspoon vegetable oil

½ teaspoon sesame oil

4 small seeded burger or
   brioche buns

1 tablespoon low-fat mayonnaise
   (see Basics section)

1. In a small bowl mix together the sesame seeds and peppers with the ground ginger and sea salt.

2. In another bowl place the finely shredded Chinese cabbage, squeeze the lemon juice over it and add the soy sauce. Place aside to stand for 15 minutes until the cabbage has softened.

3. Meanwhile, cut the tuna into 2 pieces. Roll tuna in the spice mix, pressing gently to completely coat fish with all the spice mix.

4. Preheat a small non-stick frying pan, add the vegetable and sesame oil and sear the tuna on all sides for 30 seconds so that it is still very rare. Leave tuna to rest and cool.

5. Meanwhile, slice the buns in half and toast under a hot grill.

6. Slice tuna into ¼inch (½cm) thick. Assemble the sliders by layering the tuna and cabbage mix as you like. Finish with a little light mayo to serve.

Using this recipe as a base, create your own sliders by adding chili, seaweed or pickled Japanese ginger.

Sticky pork rib with dip & slider

SERVES 4

1 tablespoon olive oil

1 garlic clove (crushed)

1 teaspoon ground coriander seeds

1 teaspoon ground fennel seeds

pinch dried chili flakes

2 tablespoons light soy sauce

2 tablespoons agave nectar

1 teaspoon English mustard powder

1 can crushed tomatoes

juice and zest of 1 lemon

2 x 10 bone small pork rib racks

black pepper

4 small seeded burger or
   brioche buns

1 small cob lettuce

1. In a small frying pan warm the olive oil and fry the crushed garlic for 1 minute until it starts to lightly colour. Add spices, the dried chili flakes, the soy sauce and the agave, cook for a further minute. Add the mustard powder and the crushed tomatoes, then the lemon juice and zest. Set aside.

2. Preheat oven to 360°F/180°C. Place a sheet of aluminium foil into the bottom of a roasting tray and put a wire rack on top. Season the rib rack with freshly ground black pepper and brush with a little olive oil. Place the ribs into the oven for 45 minutes to begin cooking.

3. After 45 minutes spread a thick coating of the sauce over the top and bottom of the ribs, then return them to the oven. Continue to cook and repeat this glazing process 3 times more, approximately 10 minutes apart.

4. For the final glaze add all the sauce and turn the oven up to 40°F/200°C, to allow the ribs to colour and become sticky. Remove from the oven and, using a small fork, pull some of the rib meat and place it between the lightly toasted buns. Top with the lettuce.

This is a light and fresh tasting sticky rib dish. The glaze can also be used for chicken, turkey or pork.

I love fresh, raw tuna. It is full of protein and rich in Omega 3. Always look for the best quality you can find. It can be used in so many great dishes.

Turkey Club Sandwich

MAKES 4 LARGE SANDWICHES

1 small red (Spanish) onion, finely
   chopped

½ clove garlic, crushed

2 avocados

sea salt and pepper

I lemon

1 tablespoon olive oil

4 rashers of bacon

8 thin slices of seeded sourdough or
   soy linseed bread

2oz (60g) butter

8oz (240g) shaved turkey breast

8 slices of reduced fat Swiss-style
   cheese

4 large eggs

½ iceberg lettuce, finely shredded

2 tablespoons low-fat mayonnaise (see
   Basics section)

sweet potato fries, optional to serve
   (not included in carb exchange)

1. Preheat oven to 360°F/180°C.

2. In a mortar and pestle, place the red onions, garlic and avocado, and pound to a rough paste as for a guacamole. Season with sea salt and pepper and a squeeze of lemon juice.

3. In a large non-stick frying pan heat the oil, add bacon and cook for 2 minutes. Place on paper towels to drain.

4. Toast half the bread in a toaster or under a hot grill, spread with butter and place on a baking tray.

5. Spread toast with a spoonful of avocado mix then layer on shaved turkey and a rasher of bacon. Top with cheese slice and place in hot oven.

6. Meanwhile, using the same pan and oil the bacon was cooked in, fry the eggs and drain any excess oil, using kitchen paper. Toast the remaining bread slices.

7. Once the cheese is melting over the bacon, remove sandwiches from the oven. Place shredded lettuce on the cheese and a dollop of mayonnaise. Place egg on mayonnaise and top with buttered toast. Skewer each side of the sandwich with small wooden skewers and cut into strips or wedges as you like.

8. Serve with sweet potato fries and tomato dipping sauce.

This is my favorite sandwich—high in protein and delicious.

Light Meals
& Salads

Chinese cabbage & Chicken salad

SERVES 4

1 x Chinese cabbage (wombok)

2 x sticks of celery

4 red radishes, finely sliced

1 x red apple

4oz (120g) roast chicken breast

½ cup low-fat cheddar cheese (grated)

DRESSING

2 tablespoons light olive oil

1 teaspoon of white wine vinegar

1 teaspoon light soy sauce

1 small knob of fresh ginger (grated)

1 tablespoon currants

sea salt and pepper

1. Wash and dry the Chinese cabbage and peel the celery. Using a sharp knife or a mandolin, cut them both as fine as possible. Place into a mixing bowl with the radishes.

2. Quarter and core the apple and slice finely. Tear the chicken breast into small pieces, then mix it and the cheese into the salad.

3. Place all of the dressing ingredients into a small jar with a lid and shake well. Pour over the salad, mix through, and serve.

You can almost eat as much of this salad as you like as it is low in calories and full of foods, such as celery and radish, that have a high water content and extremely low Gi.

Hot smoked salmon, potato lettuce & dill tip salad

SERVES 4

2 slices soy and linseed bread

½ cup small chat potatoes

2 small cos lettuces

12oz (300g) hot smoked salmon fillet

½ bunch dill tips

DRESSING

½ bunch dill tips

½ cup low-fat yoghurt

1 tablespoon low-fat mayonnaise (see Basics section)

zest and juice of 1 lime

sea salt and pepper

1 tablespoon olive oil

1. Cut the soy and linseed bread into small croutons and toast in a medium oven for 8 minutes until light brown and crisp. Allow to cool.

2. In a small bowl combine all the dressing ingredients together.

3. Cook the chat potatoes in salted water until soft and tender, keep warm.

4. Wash and trim the cos lettuce leaves then pat dry with a paper towel.

5. Prepare your serving bowls by arranging the salad leaves in them. Flake the salmon fillet over and cut the potatoes, sprinkle the croutons on the top and drizzle with the dressing.

6. Season and serve immediately.

Tip: Hot smoked salmon fillets are available at most good delis. It will look like it is already cooked, because it is.

I love this simple salad—it's crisp, light and really tasty with classic flavors.

crunchy chicken nuggets

SERVES 4

1 lb (500g) chicken breast, skin
   removed

12 fl oz (355ml) buttermilk

3oz (80g) wholewheat flour

sea salt and pepper

pinch paprika

8oz (240g) raw buckwheat

12 fl oz (355ml) vegetable or canola
   oil, for frying

DIPPING SAUCE

4oz (120g) ground almond

6oz (175g) light sour cream

1 bunch fresh chives, chopped

juice and zest of one lemon

1. Dice the chicken breast into 1inch (3cm) pieces and set aside in the fridge.

2. Pour buttermilk into a small shallow bowl. Place the flour into a separate small shallow bowl and season with sea salt and a pinch of paprika. Place the raw buckwheat into a mortar and pestle and grind lightly to just crack the kernels. Mix the ground buckwheat and almonds together and place onto a plate.

3. Coat the chicken in the flour, dip into the buttermilk and finally coat with buckwheat and almond mixture, making sure each piece is coated well. Roll gently between your palms. Place each crumbed nugget onto a tray lined with piece of baking parchment and chill in the fridge until ready to cook and serve.

4. Meanwhile, in a small bowl, combine the sour cream with the chopped fresh chives and the zest and lemon juice.

5. In a deep saucepan or deep fryer, heat the oil to 345°F/175°C and carefully deep fry the nuggets, for approximately 4 minutes. Remove from the oil onto a paper towel to drain. Serve hot with the sour cream dipping sauce.

I love deep fried chicken, and this lower Gi version is a fantastic alternative to the fast food options. The buckwheat absorbs less oil than traditional breadcrumbs.

sweet potato frittata

SERVES 4

2 medium sweet potatoes

1 tablespoon agave nectar

olive oil spray

1 tablespoon olive oil

1 red onion, finely diced

1 clove garlic, crushed

2 rashers bacon, diced

4 large eggs

4oz (120g) silken tofu

2 tablespoons light cream

sea salt and pepper

¼ bunch of flat parsley, chopped

4 egg whites

tomato or spinach salad, to serve

1. Preheat oven to 360°F/180°C. Peel and slice the sweet potato into discs approximately ¼inch (5mm) thick. Brush with the agave nectar, and spray with a little olive oil. Place on a roasting tray and bake for approximately 25 minutes until soft, cooked and golden.

2. In a small non-stick frying pan heat the oil and fry the onion, garlic and bacon together for 3 or 4 minutes. Meanwhile, line ramekins or muffin moulds with some baking parchment and spray with olive oil spray.

3. In a small bowl whisk the eggs with the tofu and cream, season with salt and pepper. Add the chopped parsley.

4. Season the inside of the moulds with salt and pepper and alternately layer the bacon mixture and sweet potato slices until almost full. Pour the egg mixture over, making sure it covers the filling.

5. Place on a baking tray and bake in the oven for 20 minutes. Test with a small knife or skewer to make sure egg is just cooked in the middle.

6. Remove from oven and allow to cool before serving with a tomato or spinach salad. Also delicious served cold.

I use a non stick individual muffin pan for this recipe, but small ramekins or moulds work just as well. They're great for school lunch boxes or fishing trips!

quinoa crusted fishcakes

MAKES 8 LARGE OR 16 SMALL CAKES

10oz (300g) potatoes, peeled and diced

10oz (300g) fresh or canned tuna

1 red onion finely chopped

1/2 tablespoon fermented chili bean
   paste

1 medium red chili

2 eggs

½ bunch Italian flat parsley, chopped

2 tablespoons of milk

sea salt and pepper

4oz (120g) white organic quinoa flakes

3oz (80g) flour

vegetable oil for frying

1. Cook the potatoes in boiling salted water until soft. Drain well and mash until smooth, then set aside to cool completely.

2. Drain the tuna, then place into a mixing bowl with the diced red onion, chili bean paste and fresh red chili. Add the cooled mashed potato, one egg and finally the chopped parsley, mix. Combine well and adjust the seasoning. The mixture should be firm and dry.

3. Divide the fishcake mixture into 8 pieces or 16 small balls and roll in your hands. Place them on a plate and refrigerate for 30 minutes to set.

4. To prepare for the coating, in a small bowl lightly whisk the remaining egg with the milk and season with a little sea salt and pepper. Place the quinoa flakes and flour into separate bowls. Roll the fishcakes firstly in the flour to lightly coat them, then dip into the egg mixture and finally press into the quinoa flakes. Shape them into small patties and using a palette knife brush off any excess flakes.

5. Pan fry the fishcakes in hot vegetable oil for 2-3 minutes each side until crisp and golden, remove from oil and drain on paper towels.

Tip: Quinoa is a highly nutritious South American seed that can be substituted for most grains. It's available from health food stores and supermarkets.

3

one ounce or half an ounce equals 15 grams one earth exchange

The flaked quinoa creates a wonderful crisp crust which is much tastier and less oily than breadcrumbs.

Barbecued Whole Shrimp, Coriander & lime

SERVES 4

1. In a mortar and pestle, pound together the red chili and garlic to a rough paste, add agave nectar and the juice of both limes.

2. Preheat a barbecue or grill plate. Brush the prawns with a little olive oil and place onto the barbecue to cook, with heads and shell on, for approximately 2 minutes each side. Allow them to char and turn a deep red. Meanwhile, cut the lemons in half and place, cut side down, onto the barbecue plate.

3. Drain and rinse the chickpeas in a colander, add to the dressing in the mortar and pestle with the remaining olive oil and the fish sauce. Stir to combine. Roughly chop the fresh coriander leaves and add half to the dressing with the sliced scallions.

4. Remove the prawns from the grill and arrange them while still hot onto a serving platter. Place grilled lemons on the side of the platter and spoon the dressing over the hot prawns.

5. Sprinkle with the remaining coriander leaves and serve.

Fresh, light and tasty, this is such a simple dish. Add extra chili to your own taste or replace shrimp with fresh grilled salmon or chicken.

spanish-style bean & sausage soup

SERVES 4

1 tablespoon olive oil

1 medium onion, finely chopped

1 clove garlic

2 x Spanish style chorizo sausages, thickly sliced

2 red peppers/capsicum, chopped

1 stalk celery, chopped

1 medium carrot, peeled and chopped

1 small leek, washed and chopped

3 Roma tomatoes

1 pinch smoked paprika

1 sprig oregano

1 sprig thyme

1 bay leaf

16 fl oz (475ml) vegetable stock

8oz (240g) borlotti beans (canned or fresh)

sea salt and pepper

crusty seeded bread, optional to serve (not included in carb exchange)

1. In a heavy-based saucepan, heat the oil and fry the onion and garlic with the sliced sausages.

2. After a minute the sausages will start to darken and the fat will render into the pan.

3. At this point add the diced vegetables, except the tomatoes, and sauté together for 5 minutes.

4. Remove the chorizo slices and set aside. Add the tomatoes, paprika and herbs. Pour in the vegetable stock and the borlotti beans and bring to a boil.

5. Reduce heat and simmer slowly for 45 minutes, until all vegetables and beans are nice and soft. Return the slices of sausages to the pot. Season with sea salt and pepper.

6. Serve hot with crusty seeded bread.

Happy family salad (swap with tuna, chicken or shrimp)

SERVES 4

1 large head of broccoli

4 red radishes

1 small green courgette/zucchini

2 stalks celery

8oz (240g) three bean mix

4 eggs (medium-hard boiled)

½ cup fresh green peas

4oz (120g) feta cheese

1 red apple

DRESSING

juice and zest of 1 lemon

juice and zest of 1 lime

1 teaspoon Dijon mustard

2 fl oz (60ml) extra virgin olive oil

sea salt and freshly ground black
   pepper

1 medium red onion, finely diced

1 medium red chili, finely chopped

Allow approximately 4oz (120g) of
   protein per person, such as cooked
   prawns/shrimp, tuna or chicken
   breast

1. In a small bowl, whisk together the dressing ingredients.

2. Prepare a bowl of iced water and bring a large pot of salted water to the boil. Trim the broccoli into small florets and drop them into the boiling water for 1 minute only. Remove from boiling water with a slotted spoon and drop immediately into the iced water for a few minutes. Once cold, drain broccoli in a strainer. (You can use raw broccoli if you prefer the crunchy texture).

3. Using a mandolin, slice radishes, zucchini and celery as thinly as possible. Place into a large serving bowl. Drizzle over half of the dressing and leave to stand for 30 minutes.

4. Drain the three bean mix and rinse in a colander. Peel the eggs and slice into quarters. Add broccoli, bean mix and fresh peas to the serving bowl and stir together. If everyone is eating the same salad, add your selected protein or divide into bowls.

5. Crumble the feta cheese over the top, slice the apple and arrange with the wedges of boiled eggs around the bowl. Drizzle with remaining dressing, season with sea salt and pepper and serve immediately.

This salad base lends itself perfectly to a range of different protein tastes. I serve the salad with sides of tuna, chicken or cooked seafood so everyone can help themselves.

Chicken, grape, pecan & pear Waldorf salad

SERVES 4

2 stalks celery

1 small cob lettuce, washed and
   drained

1 medium sized roasted chicken

3oz (80g) pecan nut halves

4oz (120g) seedless black grapes,
   sliced

1 ripe pear, thinly sliced

½ cup seeded bread croutons

DRESSING

2oz (60g) low-fat mayonnaise (see
   Basics section)

juice and zest of half a lemon

2oz (60g) light sour cream

1. In a small bowl whisk together the dressing ingredients and chill in the fridge.

2. Finely slice the celery stalks, place slices into a bowl of iced water.

3. On a serving platter scatter the cob lettuce leaves. Remove chicken meat from the bone and break into small pieces. Arrange over salad leaves. Randomly scatter pecan nuts, sliced black grapes, sliced pear and the crisp celery slices over the chicken.

4. Finish with the croutons and drizzle dressing over the top.

ROASTED Cauliflower & haloumi salad with sumac

SERVES 4

½ large cauliflower

1 cup of green beans

1 small can of chickpeas

1 knob of butter

2 tablespoons olive oil

4oz (120g) haloumi cheese

1 tablespoon sumac spice

2 tablespoons sultanas

2 tablespoons pine nuts, lightly
   toasted

sea salt and pepper

1. Preheat oven to 390°F/200°C. Cut the cauliflower into small florets and place onto a baking dish. Trim the green beans and mix with the cauliflower, add the chickpeas.

2. In a small saucepan, warm the butter and olive oil together over a low heat, drizzle over cauliflower mixture and mix through. Place in a hot oven for 25 minutes.

3. Slice the haloumi into pieces and place onto a separate baking tray, spray with a little oil and bake in the oven until brown and caramelised. Remove the cauliflower, bean and chickpeas from the oven and dust generously with the sumac. Stir through the sultanas and pine nuts then season with salt and pepper.

4. Place the cheese on the plate and spoon warm salad on the top. Squeeze some lemon juice over the salad and serve.

109

Simple and easy but great fresh flavors. Haloumi is a versatile cheese and pairs well with asparagus. Serve with chicken breast or salmon.

Rare tuna & kale salad with soy, beans & red quinoa

SERVES 4

pinch black sesame seeds

pinch white sesame seeds

½ teaspoon Sansho or Szhechuan
   pepper

pinch ground ginger

pinch sweet paprika

sea salt flakes

8oz (240g) fresh tuna fillet

½ teaspoon sesame oil

2 heads of fresh green kale

4oz (120g) fine green beans

3oz (80g) red quinoa

DRESSING

1 small piece of red chili, crushed

juice and zest of 1 lemon

1 small knob of fresh ginger, grated

1 small piece of lemongrass

1 tablespoon dark soy sauce

2 tablespoons of light olive oil

1. In a small bowl mix together the sesame seeds and Sansho pepper with the ginger, paprika and a pinch of sea salt.

2. Cut the tuna into two even-sized pieces. Season with the paprika and some sea salt. Roll tuna in the Sansho pepper mixture, pressing as much as possible of it onto the tuna.

3. Preheat a small non-stick frying pan over medium heat. Pour in sesame oil and sear the tuna on each side for only 30 seconds. Remove it from the pan and allow it to cool slightly, then roll in plastic wrap and reserve until required.

4. Wash the kale leaves and trim them into small florets, removing the stalks. Trim the green beans and cut into small batons approximately 2inches/5cm long.

5. Prepare a large bowl of iced water and also bring a large pot of salted water to the boil. Cook the kale and reserve the liquid. Refresh in in iced water. Then cook the green beans in the same water for 3 minutes, as desired.

6. In a small saucepan cook the quinoa in lightly salted water until fully absorbed and plump.

7. Place all ingredients for the dressing in a small jar and shake well. Pour the dressing over the quinoa then dry the kale in a tea-towel as best as possible. Slice the tuna as thinly as you can and mix it with the beans and the kale. Dress and serve.

Tip: Kale is classed as a superfood and a fantastic source of a variety of different vitamins.

Avocados are one
of the great
superfoods.

Lemon Chicken & power food salad

SERVES 4

2 tablespoons agave nectar

1 tablespoon hoisin sauce

juice and grated zest of 1 lemon

4 large chicken drumsticks

SALAD

3oz (80g) brown rice, cooked

3oz (80g) cannellini beans

2 scallions/green onions, finely sliced

2oz (60g) fried tofu, diced

2 tablespoons broad beans

2 tablespoons sunflower seeds

1 large ripe avocado

1 bunch baby coriander/cilantro leaves

1. In a small bowl mix together the agave nectar with the hoisin sauce and the lemon juice and zest. Place drumsticks in a large dish and brush with the mixture. Leave to marinate in the fridge for 2 hours or overnight.

2. Preheat a grill pan or barbecue and grill the drumsticks until cooked through and caramelised on the skin. Keep brushing this on as they cook. For a nice barbecue flavor, I even let the skin almost burn.

3. In a small bowl combine the salad vegetables and gently mix. Season with sea salt and pepper.

4. Mix the dressing ingredients into a small jar and shake well.

5. Serve the salad on the side with the hot sticky chicken and some lemon wedges.

I like to serve these together, but the chicken and salad both work as snacks on their own.

cucumber salad with pear & citrus dressing

SERVES 4

2 cucumbers, sliced and peeled

1 lime

sea salt

1 tablespoon hazelnuts

1 tablespoon macadamia nuts

1 bunch red radishes, quartered

1 bunch continental parsley

1 ripe pear, thinly sliced

1 bunch mint

½ bunch coriander/cilantro leaves

pinch sea salt and pepper

DRESSING

½ teaspoon yellow mustard seeds

1 tablespoon orange juice

1 tablespoon olive oil

1. Using a vegetable peeler, remove skin from cucumber. Using a mandolin, slice thinly into a bowl. Squeeze the juice of the lime over, sprinkle with sea salt flakes and leave to stand in the fridge for an hour to soften.

2. Preheat a small frying pan and dry roast the hazelnuts and macadamia nuts for approximately 3-5 minutes until they go light brown. Allow to cool and roughly chop.

3. In a larger bowl, place coriander and mint leaves, radish quarters, thinly sliced pears and the toasted nuts. Add sliced cucumbers.

4. Place dressing ingredients in a small jar and shake well. Pour the dressing over the salad, mix and serve.

Red Salad With Chorizo

SERVES 4

4oz (120g) feta cheese

pinch smoked paprika

1 tablespoon of pine nuts, lightly
   toasted

2 tablespoons of sultanas

8 small red piquillo peppers, canned

2 chorizo sausages

sea salt and pepper

1 punnet cherry tomatoes

1 small red onion

2 tablespoon olive oil

1 clove garlic

DRESSING

pinch smoked paprika

1 tablespoon red wine vinegar

1 tablespoon almond meal

2 small piquillo peppers

1 tablespoon olive oil

1. Preheat oven to 360°F/180°C. In a small bowl cream the feta with a spoon and season with a pinch of smoked paprika. Add the toasted pine nuts and the sultanas and mix well.

2. Using a teaspoon, fill the peppers with the feta stuffing mixture, then lay them onto a baking tray. Bake in oven for 5 minutes until warmed through.

3. Meanwhile, slice the chorizo on an angle and grill them in a small pan or on a hot barbecue plate for 2 minutes each side.

4. Place all the dressing ingredients into a blender and pulse together.

5. Arrange cherry tomatoes, onion, peppers and chorizo onto a warm plate and drizzle with dressing.

Chorizo sausage is made from pork and will give a wonderful Spanish flavor to this dish.

Rare beef, tuna & green bean salad with manchego & capers

SERVES 4

4oz (120g) tuna fillet (fresh,
    or canned in spring water)
sea salt and pepper
8oz (240g) centre cut beef fillet
1 tablespoon olive oil
½ cup low-fat mayonnaise (see Basics
    section)
1 clove of garlic
1 lemon
4oz (120g) green beans
2oz (60g) Manchego
    or parmesan cheese
1 tablespoon baby capers
lemon wedges, to serve

1. Preheat oven to 360°F/180°C. If the tuna is fresh, season it with some salt and pepper. Heat a small non-stick frying pan over a high heat and cook tuna for 1 minute each side, leaving the middle pink. Allow to rest and to cool, then flake it into a small bowl using a table fork. If you are using canned tuna, drain and place the tuna into a small bowl.

2. Season the beef fillet and cook in a hot non-stick frying pan with a little olive oil for 2 minutes each side to seal it, making sure to turn onto all sides.

3. Place beef on a baking tray and cook in oven for approximately 5 minutes. Try to leave it rare, then set aside to rest and cool for 5 minutes.

4. Meanwhile, combine the mayonnaise with the tuna, season with salt and pepper, finely grate a small amount of the garlic and some lemon zest into the bowl with the tuna and mix well.

5. Trim the ends from the green beans and blanch in boiling salted water for 1 minute then refresh in iced water until cold. Slice the beans thinly lengthways.

6. To serve, slice the beef as thinly as possible and place onto serving plates. Add a spoon of the tuna and arrange the green beans on the top. Shave or grate the cheese over the top and sprinkle a few capers around. Drizzle with a small amount of olive oil and serve with a wedge of lemon.

Why not serve this dish as a centrepiece for a brunch or even make it smaller for a great appetizer?

cold set chicken pasta salad

SERVES 4-6

1 medium-sized whole fresh chicken
   (I prefer organic)

1 onion

1 stalk celery

2 fresh bay leaves

8 black peppercorns

4oz (120g) wholemeal spiral or penne
   pasta

2 tablespoons low-fat Greek style
   yoghurt

2 tablespoons low-fat mayonnaise (see
   Basics section)

2 lemons

Salt and pepper

1 small jar of marinated artichokes
   (cut in quarters)

2 tablespoons whole almonds, finely
   shredded

1. Place the chicken into a large pot of salted water with the peeled onion, celery, bay leaves and peppercorns. Bring to the boil and simmer slowly for approximately 45 minutes.

2. Prepare a large bowl or pot (large enough for the whole chicken to fit into) full of iced water. Carefully remove the whole chicken from the pot and put it directly into the iced water and allow to cool completely.

3. Cook the pasta in salted water until al dente, and refresh under cold water. Allow to drain.

4. In a small bowl, mix the yoghurt, low-fat mayonnaise and the zest and juice of one lemon. Season with salt and pepper.

5. Remove the skin from the chicken and pick the breast and leg meat from the frame, tearing in small pieces and placing into a bowl.

6. In a separate bowl, mix the pasta with the chicken and artichokes, sprinkle the almonds on the top and serve with the dressing on the side.

This method of cooking chicken creates the most flavorsome and moist cold chicken. It's ideal for any type of cold chicken dish, sandwich or salad.

sweet potato fries

SERVES 4

20 fl oz (600ml) vegetable oil
12oz (300g) sweet potatoes, peeled
pinch sea salt flakes

1. In a deep saucepan heat the oil to 300°F/150°C, making sure the oil does not go over half way up the side of the pan.

2. Cut the sweet potatoes into long stalks and place carefully into the oil. Keep cooking at 300°F/150°C for 3 minutes until the fries begin to soften, but do not darken.

3. Carefully drain and remove from the oil (at this stage you may cool fries and keep in a fridge for later).

4. To serve, heat the oil to 350°F/175C and carefully place the fries back into the oil to cook. They will go golden and crispy (approximately 2-3 minutes). Remove from hot oil and immediately place fries onto paper towels to drain.

5. Allow the oil to cool, then strain through a fine strainer. Season the hot fries with sea salt flakes and serve.

Regular potato fries should be off your menu, but if you occasionally feel the urge, these fries are higher in fibre, lower Gi and full of nutrients.

Tataki of salmon with pomegranate, citrus & garden herbs

SERVES 4

4oz (120g) fresh salmon fillet

1 teaspoon olive oil

½ pomegranate

2oz (60g) natural yoghurt

juice and zest of 1 lemon

pepper and sea salt

selection of baby herbs

1 mandarin

1. Slice the salmon fillet as thinly as possible and lay onto a sheet of plastic wrap or greaseproof paper. Lightly rub with a little olive oil and lay another sheet of greaseproof paper on the top. Using a rolling pin or a clean bottle, roll the salmon fillet as thinly as possible and place into the fridge until required.

2. Remove the seeds from the pomegranate by half hitting the bottom of it with a wooden spoon and allowing the seeds to fall out into a bowl.

3. Whisk together the yoghurt with a squeeze of lemon juice and a little of the zest.

4. To serve, remove salmon from the fridge and take off the top layer of paper (see picture insert). Rub salmon with remaining olive oil and season generously with pepper and a pinch of sea salt. Pinch the salmon between your fingers lightly and drop flesh randomly onto your serving plate.

5. Sprinkle the pomegranate seeds around and drizzle with yoghurt dressing. Finish with herbs and mandarin segments.

Tataki means to flatten or hammer.

sweet chicken skewers

SERVES 4

2 large chicken breasts

2 tablespoons agave nectar

3 tablespoons light soy sauce

juice and zest of one lemon

small knob of fresh ginger, grated

sesame seeds and fresh herbs, to serve

8 bamboo skewers

1. Soak the bamboo skewers in cold water for 30 minutes. Cut the chicken breast into small strips.

2. Combine all other ingredients in a small bowl. Thread the chicken dice onto the skewers and brush with the marinade mixture. Cook on a hot barbecue plate or in a non-stick frying pan. Don't keep turning but allow skewers to caramelise and even char on the edges, this should only take approximately 5-6 minutes to cook.

3. Sprinkle with some sesame seeds and fresh herbs.

Great for an outdoor barbecue, these skewers also work well as a quick snack or can be served cold in packed lunches.

Mini fish tacos with soy, avocado & lime

MAKES 8 SMALL TACOS

4oz (120g) fresh kingfish fillet, or
   other white fish fillet

1 small scallion/shallot, finely diced

1 small piece of lemongrass, finely
   chopped

1 medium red chili, finely chopped

juice and zest of 1 lime

½ avocado

sea salt and pepper

1 small piece of fresh ginger, grated

½ teaspoon soy sauce

½ bunch fresh cilantro/coriander
   leaves

8 small crisp taco shells

1. Using a large knife, finely chop the kingfish and place into a small bowl with the scallions, lemongrass and chili.

2. Cut the lime in half. Cut one half into 4 wedges. Zest and juice the other half onto the kingfish.

3. In a separate bowl mash the avocado with a fork to a smooth paste and season with sea salt and pepper.

4. Add the ginger, soy sauce and half of the cilantro to the kingfish. Taste and adjust the seasoning.

5. To assemble, place small taco shells in a stand or between 2 small plates. Spoon in marinated kingfish mixture, top with a teaspoonful of avocado, scatter cilantro leaves over and serve.

Tacos are the perfect finger food for parties, and a great snack to have when you are watching a movie with the family.

.5

an ounce or half 13grams equals one carb exchange

Barbecued Salmon
Sang Choy Bau

SERVES 4

2 teaspoons soy sauce

1 teaspoon agave nectar

2 salmon steaks

pinch ground ginger

1 tablespoon vegetable oil

½ bunch scallions/shallots, sliced

1 red pepper/capsicum diced

2 tablespoons corn kernels

1 cup brown rice, cooked

1 pinch dried chili flakes (optional)

1 cup bean sprouts

1 pinch ground ginger

1 lemon

1 large lettuce (iceberg, cob or
   romaine)

1. In a small bowl mix together half of the soy sauce and agave nectar and brush over the salmon steaks. Dust them with the ground ginger and place in the fridge for at least 30 minutes or overnight.

2. Warm oil in a wok or large non-stick frying pan, sear the salmon steaks for 2 minutes each side and remove to a plate. After resting for a minute or two, use a fork to flake salmon into small pieces and set aside.

3. In the same hot wok, add the scallions, red pepper and corn kernels, then stir-fry together for 3 minutes. Add the rice, chili flakes if using, and a tablespoon of water. Add the salmon and any juices on the plate and stir-fry together for a one minute. It should be moist but not glugging together. Add bean sprouts. Add a squeeze of fresh lemon juice, season and serve in the leaves of cob, romaine or iceberg lettuce.

A great, sharing family dish for everyone.

Mains

Roasted Chicken, bean & Chipotle bake with corn

SERVES 4

1 lemon

1 large fresh chicken

1 tablespoon olive oil

sea salt and pepper

CHIPOTLE BAKE

2oz (60g) olive oil

1 medium red/Spanish onion, finely
  chopped

1 clove garlic

½ teaspoon chipotle chili paste

8oz (240g) cooked cannellini beans

6oz (175g) canned crushed tomatoes

1 fl oz (30ml) white wine vinegar

1 teaspoon agave nectar

sea salt and pepper

1 fresh corn cob or small can of
  kernels

2 tablespoons dried breadcrumbs

2oz (60g) grated parmesan cheese

1. Preheat oven to 360°F/180°C. Slice the lemon thinly and using your finger, place under the skin on the breast of the chicken. Rub the chicken with the olive oil, then season with sea salt and freshly ground black pepper. Place onto a baking dish and cook for approximately 45 minutes. Meanwhile, prepare the bean and chipotle bake.

2. In a saucepan, heat the olive oil and fry together the onion and the garlic for 2 minutes. Add the chipotle paste and the cannellini beans and cook for a further 2 minutes. Add the tomatoes, white wine vinegar and agave nectar, bring to the boil and cover with a lid. Reduce heat and simmer for 15 minutes until a thick and rich sauce begins to form. Season with sea salt and pepper to taste.

3. Pour bean mixture into a shallow baking dish and sprinkle over corn kernels, then breadcrumbs and the grated parmesan cheese. Place this dish in a medium oven for 35 minutes until the top is golden brown and crusty. To serve, slice the chicken onto your plate and serve with the hot bake.

Tip: Prepare the bake in advance and cook it in the oven with the chicken.

A hearty winter warmer that will satisfy everyone.

seafood & sweet potato curry with tofu

SERVES 4

4oz (120g) whitefish fillets

4oz (120g) tuna steak

1 small can Thai green curry paste

2 medium sweet potatoes, peeled and
    washed

1 teaspoon vegetable oil

1 small knob ginger, crushed

1 clove garlic

1 medium onion, finely sliced

20 fl oz (600ml) vegetable stock

1 tablespoon agave nectar

4oz (120g) cooked prawns

4oz (120g) green beans

1 bunch bok choy

1 small can bamboo shoots

3 fl oz (100ml) light coconut cream

½ bunch fresh basil

4oz (120g) silken tofu

2 teaspoons fish sauce

1 lemon

steamed low Gi rice, to serve

mint leaves to garnish

1. Rub the swordfish and tuna steaks with some of the green curry paste and place in the fridge for 30 minutes.

2. Dice the sweet potatoes into cubes, approximately ½inch (1cm) squares.

3. In a medium-sized saucepan heat a teaspoon of vegetable oil and fry the crushed ginger, garlic, onion and 1 tablespoon of green curry paste—add more if you like it really spicy.

4. Add the sweet potato, vegetable stock and agave nectar, bring to the boil and reduce to a simmer for 15 minutes. Dice the swordfish and tuna into ½inch (1cm) cubes.

5. Heat a small frying pan and sear the whitefish and tuna for 1 minute each side. Remove from the pan and allow to cook through, then using a fork, break into small bite-sized pieces.

6. Add the coconut cream and basil leaves to the curry, then stir in the prawns, seafood and vegetables. Finally add the tofu, bring up to heat and season with the fish sauce and lemon juice. To reduce the carb exchange, serve with a small amount of some low Gi rice or even just a nice salad.

People with diabetes should avoid coconut cream and palm-sugar based curries. My tasty and healthier alternative is a great choice for those curry cravings.

MY mac & cheese

SERVES 8

3 cloves garlic

2 bay leaves

1 large cauliflower

8oz (240g) wholewheat elbow
   macaroni pasta

sea salt and pepper

1 tablespoon olive oil

1 tablespoon Dijon mustard

3oz (80g) light sour cream

4oz (120g) fresh full cream ricotta
   cheese

4oz (120g) natural Greek style yoghurt

juice of 1 lemon

4oz (120g) honey roasted or smoked
   gypsy ham (roughly diced)

4oz (120g) low-fat cheddar cheese

2oz (60g) grated parmesan cheese

½ cup soy and linseed breadcrumbs

salad or green beans, to serve

1. Bring a large pot of salted water to the boil, add the garlic cloves and the bay leaves then simmer for two minutes. Add the roughly chopped cauliflower and simmer for approximately 6 minutes until the cauliflower is soft.

2. Once cooked, carefully drain and retain the liquid, put it in the same pan and bring back to the boil, add the macaroni and cook for approximately 10 minutes until cooked al dente. Once again retain the liquid.

3. Remove the bay leaves and discard. Place the garlic cloves and the mustard into a blender. Add the sour cream, ricotta cheese and the yoghurt and pulse to a paste. Add the lemon juice.

4. Place a large baking dish over a high heat and add the tablespoon of olive oil. Add diced ham and the drained cauliflower and fry for 2 minutes then add a ladle of the drained cooking liquid and the cooked macaroni. Bring to a high simmer.

5. Stir in the ricotta cheese mixture, add the cheddar and parmesan cheeses. Stir well until they melt to form a sauce (it with thicken once baked in the oven).

6. Sprinkle the soy and linseed breadcrumbs on the top and then bake in a medium oven for 25 minutes until golden brown and crunchy on the top. Serve with a big salad or green beans.

It's the cauliflower in the sauce that makes this such a popular and unusual take on a classic.

Braised Sticky Short ribs With Steel-cut oats

SERVES 4

1 tablespoon olive oil

2 lb (1kg) short trimmed beef ribs

2 pints (1.2 litres) beef stock

2 tablespoons agave nectar

1 cup of balsamic vinegar

1 cinnamon stick

1 lemon, halved

1 small knob of butter

½ onion, finely chopped

4oz (120g) celeriac, peeled and finely sliced

4oz (120g) steel-cut oats

16 fl oz (475ml) hot vegetable stock

sea salt and pepper

1. In a heavy-based saucepan heat the olive oil and sear the beef ribs on both sides. Remove ribs to an ovenproof dish and allow to rest.

2. In a separate pan, bring the beef stock to the boil with the agave nectar, balsamic vinegar, cinnamon and lemon. Pour liquid over the beef rib, bring to a rolling boil and cover with a lid.

3. Place the beef in the dish into a medium 360°F/180°C oven and cook for 1½ hours.

4. Remove beef ribs carefully from the liquid (They should be very soft and tender falling apart almost), strain the liquid into a clean saucepan and place onto the heat to reduce by two thirds, until it is a concentrated dark glaze. Brush glaze onto the beef ribs and place them into a medium oven for 30 minutes. Continue to brush more glaze on every 10 minutes until ribs become rich and sticky. Keep ribs warm for serving.

5. In a saucepan, melt the butter and fry the onion and celeriac together for 2 minutes then add the steel-cut oats and gradually stir in the hot vegetable stock. This will thicken quickly, so keep adding the stock until the oats are fully absorbed and soft.

6. To serve, adjust the seasoning of the oats and brush the hot beef ribs one more time with the glaze.

148

Oats are not just an ingredient for breakfast, they also make a great side dish.

Barbecue rib steak, with fresh horseradish & chili

SERVES 4

4 x 12oz (300g) rib eye steaks on the
    bone
1 tablespoon olive oil
sea salt and pepper
2oz (60g) piece of fresh horseradish
1 cup of red mustard or red frill leaves
½ cup pickled chili (see Basics section)

1. Preheat a barbecue plate or skillet pan.

2. Rub the steaks with a little olive oil and season with sea salt and pepper. Place the steaks onto the hot grill plate and cook to your liking. Remove from the grill plate and allow the steaks to rest for 2 minutes before serving them.

3. Slice the beef onto the plate. Sprinkle the red frill leaves and loosely scatter the pickled chilie salsa over as well. Finally using a microplane-style grater, grate the fresh horseradish on the top.

slow cooked lamb shanks with Italian vegetables & sage

SERVES 4

4 x 12oz (300g) French trimmed lamb
    shanks

sea salt and pepper

2 tablespoons of olive oil

1 medium onion, finely chopped

1 clove fresh garlic

1 glass of red wine

1 sprig of fresh rosemary

1 punnet of cherry tomatoes

1 medium can crushed tomatoes

1 medium sized green courgette/
    zucchini, thinly sliced

6oz (175g) buckwheat cooked in
    boiling salted water

12 large green olives

1 bunch fresh sage

selection of seasonal green vegetables

1. Preheat oven to 360°F/180°C degrees and heat a large earthenware casserole dish on the stovetop.

2. Season the lamb shanks with sea salt and pepper. Add the olive oil to the dish and sear the lamb shanks for 3 minutes on all sides.

3. Remove the lamb shanks and add the chopped onion and the garlic. Cook for 2-3 minutes until softened then add the red wine and the sprig of rosemary. Reduce wine by half, add cherry tomatoes and crushed tomatoes. Return the shanks to the pan and bring to the boil.

4. Cover dish with some foil and a lid and place in a medium oven (360°F/180°C degrees) for 1 hour and 30 minutes.

5. After 1 hour 20 minutes remove from the oven and with a small knife test that the meat is cooked through and falling off the bone. Depending on the actual size of the shanks they may need up to another 30 minutes to cook.

6. Carefully remove the shanks from the sauce and set aside. Add the sliced green zucchini, buckwheat and green olives to the sauce and stir through, adjust seasoning with sea salt and pepper.

7. Spoon the sauce over the shanks and garnish with the fresh sage leaves. Serve with steamed seasonal vegetables.

one ounce or half an ounce equals 15grams or one carb exchange

2

This combination of flavors works so well together. The cooked meat can also be picked off the bone and served in a sandwich or flaked over a salad or even in a pasta dish.

crusty chicken schnitzel

SERVES 4

2 tablespoons pumpkin seeds (pepitas)

2 tablespoons sunflower seeds

2 tablespoons white sesame seeds

½ cup of almond meal

½ cup of wholemeal flour

sea salt and pepper

2 eggs

4 x 4oz (120g) skinless chicken breast
    fillets

2 tablespoons vegetable oil for shallow
    frying

2 lemons

green salad leaves to serve

1. Place the pumpkin seeds and the sunflower seeds in a blender, add the almond meal and pulse together for a minute or two. Don't let the mix become too fine, I like to leave it nice and crunchy. Add the sesame seeds and mix through, then pour mixture into a small flat bowl.

2. Place the flour into another small flat bowl and season with sea salt and pepper. Break the eggs into another small flat bowl add a tablespoon of water and lightly whisk with a fork.

3. Lay chicken breasts on a cutting board and slice through the centre to open them up. Using a large knife lightly batter the chicken breast fillets so they become flat.

4. Lightly coat the chicken breast fillets in the seasoned flour, then pass through the egg mixture and finally into the almond meal and seed mixture.

5. Preheat the vegetable oil in a non-stick frying pan and cook the chicken on each side, until crumbs are golden brown and crispy and chicken is cooked through. Remove from the pan and drain on a piece of kitchen paper. Serve with green salad and fresh cut lemon.

spice-crusted skillet fish with walnut pesto

SERVES 4

4 x 4oz (120g) fish fillets (kingfish,
    salmon, snapper or tuna)
2oz (60g) low-fat feta cheese

SPICE CRUST
1 tablespoon cumin seeds
1 tablespoon fennel seeds
½ teaspoon dried chili flakes
½ teaspoon smoked paprika pepper
2 tablespoon olive oil

WALNUT PESTO
3oz (80g) walnut pieces
1 tablespoon pine nuts
1 medium red onion (finely diced)
2 cloves garlic, chopped
2 tablespoons olive oil
1 tablespoon parmesan cheese
1 sprig lemon thyme
2 tablespoons red wine vinegar (good
    quality)
sea salt and pepper

1. For spice crust, use a mortar and pestle to grind spices together with the oil. Rub onto fish fillets, cover with plastic wrap and rest for 1 hour in the fridge.

2. Place the walnut pieces and the pine nuts onto a roasting tray and cook in a medium oven at 360°F/180°C degrees until lightly browned and toasted.

3. Preheat a small non-stick frying pan and fry the onion and garlic in the olive oil until softened. Allow to cool.

4. In a blender, mix the walnuts with the cooked onion, garlic, lemon thyme and parmesan cheese. Add the red wine vinegar and pulse to a pesto texture.

5. Preheat a heavy skillet or frypan, and cook the spice-crusted fish for 2 minutes on each side, allowing the spices to caramelise. Serve with some of the walnut pesto.

Walnuts are high in protein and fibre. The spices cook at same time as the fish, which adds great flavor.

159

Steamed fish fillet with baby spinach & dukkah eggs

SERVES 4

4 x 4oz (120g) firm fish fillets
    (snapper, kingfish)

½ teaspoon sea salt flakes

½ teaspoon freshly ground black
    pepper

2 cups fresh baby spinach

6 large fresh eggs (cooked in shell for
    5 minutes from boiling)

DUKKAH SPICE MIX

½ cup ground hazelnuts

2 tablespoons sesame seeds

2 tablespoons ground cumin

1 tablespoon ground coriander

1 tablespoon ground fennel seeds

pinch ground nutmeg

pinch ground cloves

1. Preheat oven to 360°F/180°C. Mix all the dukkah spice ingredients together in a bowl and pour onto a baking sheet. Place in the oven for 6 minutes, mix through with a fork and allow to cool. Keep in an airtight jar for up to 2 weeks.

2. Place a bamboo steamer over a large pan of boiling water (or use an electric steamer if you prefer). Season the snapper fillets with sea salt and freshly ground black pepper and put them onto a small plate, or a piece of greased baking parchment.

3. Put the spinach into a small bowl and season with a pinch of sea salt.

4. Place the snapper into the steamer to cook. After 3 minutes place the spinach into the steamer and continue to cook both spinach and snapper for a further 3 minutes until cooked through and firm to touch. Allow fish to rest in the warm steamer.

5. Peel the boiled eggs and slice into wedges. Drain any excess water from the spinach. Arrange on a plate with the snapper and wedges of egg. Sprinkle with plenty of the dukkah and serve.

The combination of ingredients makes this Angela's personal favorite and most requested dish for me to make at home!

steamed mussels in a bag with fennel

SERVES 4

1 onion, finely sliced

1 fennel bulb, finely sliced

2lb (1kg) live black mussels

2 fresh bay leaves

1 clove of garlic

fresh black pepper

½ glass white wine

½ bunch dill or fennel tips

1. Preheat the oven to 360°F/180°C. Place the sliced onions and fennel into a small saucepan full of water and bring to the boil. Rinse under cold water and drain.

2. Wash and clean the mussels making sure all of the small beards and any barnacles have been removed. Lay a large sheet of aluminium foil on a bench and cover with a piece of greaseproof paper of similar size. Place the foil and paper sheets over a bowl or colander and push down in the middle to form a bowl shape.

3. Place mussels, blanched fennel, onions, fresh bay leaves, garlic and a few black peppercorns into the foil and paper then pour in wine.

4. Using both hands, draw the side together to form a bag and twist the top to seal the bag, tie with a piece of butchers twine.

5. Place bag into the oven for 15 minutes. The mussels will steam open and form a light sauce.

6. Open the bag at the table and sprinkle the dill tips on the top and serve with some finger bowls and hot bread or sweet potato chips.

You can make this dish in advance.
Prepare it to the point where the bag
is tied and keep in the fridge until
required.

High protein spaghetti bolognese

SERVES 4

3 tablespoons olive oil

8oz beef scotch fillet,
    diced ¼ in/5mm

8oz (240g) pork loin fillet
    diced ¼ in/5mm

1 onion, chopped

1 garlic clove

a splash of red wine

4oz (120g) Roma tomatoes, diced

1 punnet cherry tomatoes

1 can crushed tomatoes

1 pint (600ml) vegetable stock

1 sprig of lemon thyme

4oz (120g) tofu fried and
    diced ¼ in/5mm

Sea salt and black pepper

3 slices soy and linseed bread

3oz (80g) grated parmesan cheese

8oz (240g) whole wheat or
    gluten-free spaghetti

1. Preheat a large frypan or casserole dish, add half the olive oil and fry together the seasoned diced beef and pork loin, sauté for 3 minutes, then add the onions and garlic cook for another 2 minutes. Add a splash of red wine and reduce by half. Add the chopped Roma, cherry tomatoes and crushed tomatoes, with the vegetable stock.

2. Drop in the sprig of lemon thyme, cover with a lid and simmer for 45 minutes. Check that the meat is tender using a small knife, and add the diced tofu.

3. Adjust the seasoning with salt and pepper or add dried chili if you prefer, then reduce the sauce to a thick texture.

4. Toast the soy and linseed bread and put into a blender with the parmesan cheese. Pulse together for 1 minute to a coarse crumb. Add a tablespoon of olive oil, pour on to a baking tray and bake in a medium oven at 360°F/180°C for 3 minutes.

5. Cook the spaghetti in boiling salted water as per packet directions, until al dente. Drain and place spaghetti in a large bowl in the middle of the table with the rich sauce on the top and sprinkle with the parmesan crumbs.

I always try to have a higher percentage of meat, but you can adjust to your liking or even make this with tofu.

Massive meatball bake

SERVES 4

MEATBALLS

6oz (175g) lean lamb or hamburger
   mince

6oz (175g) lean pork mince

1 onion, finely diced

2 tablespoon pine nuts, lightly toasted

1 clove garlic, crushed

3oz (80g) low-fat feta cheese,
   crumbled

2 tablespoons fresh basil leaves,
   shredded

2 tablespoons fresh parsley leaves,
   shredded

2 egg whites

½ cup wholemeal breadcrumbs

½ teaspoon English mustard

1 teaspoon Worcestershire sauce

sea salt and pepper

pinch ground nutmeg

3oz (80g) mozzarella cheese, grated

SAUCE

3 tablespoons olive oil

1 clove garlic, chopped

1 medium onion, diced

1 medium eggplant/aubergine, diced

1 green courgette/zucchini, diced

2 ripe tomatoes, diced

1 tablespoon white wine vinegar

sea salt and pepper

1. In a mixing bowl combine all of the ingredients together (except for the mozzarella) and mix well. Using your hands and a bowl of cold water, wet your hands and then roll the meatballs into 12 pieces the approximate size of a golf ball, then set aside.

2. Preheat an oven to 360°F/180°C. Brush the inside of a roasting dish with a little vegetable oil and place the meatballs into it. Bake in the oven for 20 minutes.

3. Remove meatballs from the oven and sprinkle with grated mozzarella cheese, and bake for a further 5 minutes to melt the cheese. Meanwhile, prepare your sauce.

4. In a non-stick frying pan, heat the olive oil and fry the garlic and onion together for 2 minutes. Then add the eggplant and zucchini and cook for 4 minutes until soft then add tomatoes and vinegar. Simmer for 10 minutes and season to taste. Spoon meatballs into bowls, spoon over sauce and serve.

I use meatballs as the base and change the sauce to suit the season, such as mushrooms in autumn.

A healthy meal on a pizza

SERVES 6

FOR THE BASE

1 large pita or Lebanese bread

½ cup Napolitana sauce

3oz (80g) button mushrooms, finely
sliced

1 medium sliced green courgette/
zucchini, finely sliced

2 eschallots/French shallots or red
onions

4oz (120g) small bocconcini cheese

½ punnet grape or cherry tomatoes

½ bunch fresh parsley

½ cup low-fat mozzarella cheese,
grated

FOR THE TOPPING

2 cups baby spinach or rocket leaves

2 ripe avocados, diced

3oz (80g) low-fat feta cheese,
crumbled

4 bacon rashers, grilled

½ punnet grape or cherry tomatoes

4 red radishes, finely sliced

½ cup of fresh herbs

1 lemon

2 tablespoons of olive oil

1. Preheat oven to 360°F/180°C degrees. Place the bread on a large baking tray, spread a little of the tomato sauce over and then in a random fashion sprinkle the sliced mushrooms, zucchini and eschallots over the top. Chop the bocconcini, grape tomatoes and parsley and scatter them randomly over the bread. Sprinkle with the grated mozzarella and season with sea salt and pepper. Bake in the oven for 12 minutes.

2. Meanwhile, place the rocket leaves into a mixing bowl and mix with the remaining topping ingredients like a mixed salad, season well and dress with a little olive oil and squeeze of lemon.

3. Remove the hot bread from the oven and allow to cool for 2 minutes. Spoon the salad topping onto the bread. Cut into large wedges, season and serve

This dish can easily be changed to suit your taste. Simply add grilled chicken, sliced steak or grilled shrimp.

Sweet Treats, Desserts & Bakes

Not-so-naughty chocolate cake

MAKES ONE LARGE 3-LAYERED CAKE. SERVES 12

10oz (300g) fresh full cream
　　ricotta cheese
4 fl oz (120ml) fresh milk (2% fat)
1oz (30g) unsweetened pure
　　cocoa powder
2 tablespoons agave nectar
2oz (60g) butter
3 large fresh eggs
6oz (175g) self-raising/bakers
　　flour
½ teaspoon bicarbonate of soda
2oz (60g) ground almonds
Fresh berries or figs and icing
　　sugar to serve

CHOCOLATE TOPPING
4 fl oz (120ml) light cream
2 drops vanilla essence
1 teaspoon agave nectar
4oz (120g) dark chocolate, 71%
　　cocoa

4fl oz (120ml) cream, lightly
　　whisked with 1 teaspoon
　　agave nectar

1. Preheat oven to 360°F/180°C. In a large mixing bowl or electric kitchen mixer place the ricotta and, using the beater attachment, mix vigorously for 3 minutes until very smooth.

2. Mix the cocoa into a small amount of the milk, then warm it with the remaining milk and agave nectar. Stir in the butter to melt then allow to cool.

3. In a separate bowl, lightly whisk eggs with a fork.

4. Sift the flour, bicarbonate of soda and ground almonds onto a sheet of baking parchment.

5. With the mixer on a medium speed, gradually add the egg to the ricotta then add the milk and butter mixture. Add the almonds and flour mix together and combine. Do not over mix at this point.

6. Grease and line a 8inch/20cm cake tin with baking parchment, bake in oven for 30 minutes, do not open oven during cooking.

7. Invert cake on to a cooling wire rack and allow to cool.

8. To make the chocolate topping: in a small pan warm the cream, vanilla and agave nectar. Remove from heat and add the chocolate. Stir until mixed and allow to cool. Do not put in the fridge.

9. Using a large bread knife, slice the cake into three pieces horizontally. Then spread each layer with some of the chocolate topping, the whisked cream and the fresh fruit. Finally garnish the top with some dark chocolate shavings and a very light dusting of icing sugar. To make chocolate shavings scrape a sharp knife over a bar of (room temperature) dark chocolate or use a vegetable peeler

A low-fat, low Gi, high protein, low sugar chocolate cake.

Peach, pear & raspberry semi-freddo

SERVES 4

4oz (120g) canned pears, drained to produce 2 fl oz (60ml) syrup
½ punnet fresh raspberries
2 tablespoons cornflour
2 tablespoons agave nectar
4oz (120g) canned peaches, drained
8 fl oz milk
6oz (175g) natural yoghurt

1. Warm the pear syrup and pour over the fresh raspberries. Place in the fridge to cool.

2. Mix the cornflour, agave nectar and 2 tablespoons of the milk.

3. Bring remaining milk to the boil and stir in the cornflour mixture stirring well until it thickens. Remove from the heat, cover and allow to cool.

4. In a blender place the pears and peaches. Drain the syrup from the raspberries and set them aside.

5. Blend the pears and peaches until smooth, then add the cold milk custard mixture and combine together.

6. Add the natural yoghurt and mix well.

7. Line a small loaf tin or ramekin dishes with plastic wrap and pour in the mixture.

8. Drop one or two raspberries into each dish and place into the freezer for at least 3 hours to set.

9. Remove from the freezer for 45 minutes before serving.

This is a refreshing light alternative to ice cream.

Blueberry & hazelnut muffins

MAKES 12 MUFFINS

10oz (300g) full cream ricotta
    cheese

2 tablespoons agave nectar

2oz (60g) butter

4 fl oz (120ml) milk

3 large fresh eggs

6oz (175g) self-raising/bakers
    flour

2oz (60g) ground almonds

2oz (60g) ground hazelnuts

½ teaspoon bicarbonate soda

½ cup fresh blueberries

3oz (80g) crème fraîche
    (optional)

1. Preheat oven to 360°F/180°C. In the large bowl of an electric mixer place the ricotta and beat with the beater attachment vigorously for 3 minutes until it becomes very smooth.

2. In a small saucepan, melt the agave nectar with the butter and the milk. Take off the heat and allow to cool.

3. Break the eggs into another small bowl and lightly whisk with a fork.

4. Sift together the flour, ground almonds, ground hazelnuts and the bicarbonate of soda.

5. Reduce the mixer speed to slow then gradually add the eggs and the milk mixture to the ricotta. Then add the dry ingredients and combine well but do not over mix. Carefully add the blueberries, trying not to break them up.

6. Lightly grease and flour a 12-hole muffin tray and drop large spoonfuls of the mixture in, filling approximately ¾ of the way up.

7. Bake in oven for 20 minutes. Remove muffin tray from the oven and allow to cool for a minute or two before removing from the tray. Serve with some crème fraîche or sugar-free fruit spread.

peanut butter & chocolate mini tartlets

MAKES APPROXIMATELY 20 SMALL TARTLETS, 2 PER PORTION

½ packet of filo pastry
2oz (60g) butter, melted
1 tablespoon agave nectar
6 fl oz (175ml) light cream
½ teaspoon vanilla essence
4oz (120g) dark chocolate
    buttons
    (71%chocolate)
3oz (80g) low-fat crunchy peanut
    butter
1 tablespoon dark cocoa
fresh raspberries

1. Preheat oven to 360°F/180°C. Brush a sheet of filo pastry with melted butter and place another sheet of filo on top. Repeat with two other layers. Cut layered filo using a pastry ring to fit the size of the small tartlet moulds, approximately 1inch (3cm) in diameter. Line the moulds with the filo and some baking parchment discs, then place some rice or beans inside. Repeat with another 2 layers.

2. Blind bake pastry in the oven for 3 minutes, remove from oven and discard the baking beans and paper. Return pastry shells to the oven and bake for a further 3 minutes until golden and crisp. Remove from the oven and allow to cool.

3. In a small saucepan, bring the agave and the cream to the boil with the vanilla essence. Place chocolate buttons into a bowl and pour over hot cream mix. Stir together until smooth. Set aside and allow to cool, but do not refrigerate.

4. If chocolate hasn't melted enough microwave it briefly.

5. To make the tartlets, place some peanut butter in the bottom of each one and pipe or spoon the chocolate mixture on the top. Dust with a little dark cocoa and finish with a raspberry or a strawberry.

182

Poached Strawberry & Rhubarb jelly

SERVES 6

6g agar agar or gelatine
   jelly crystals (diluted as per
   instructions on packet)
1 bunch rhubarb
2 punnets strawberries
1 pint (600ml) of water
1 small knob of fresh ginger
6oz (180g) light cream
   sweetened with a little agave
   nectar
chocolate biscuits

1. In a small saucepan bring the water and agave nectar to the boil with the ginger.

2. Trim the rhubarb with a vegetable peeler and cut it into 1inch (3cm) batons.

3. Trim the stalks from the top of the strawberries then drop both the rhubarb pieces and the whole strawberries into the syrup and simmer for 1 minute only. Remove saucepan from the heat and allow it to cool with fruit in the syrup. This will allow the syrup to take the colour and flavor of the fruit.

4. Carefully remove the fruit and drain in a small colander. Remove the ginger at this point.

5. Strain the syrup and return it to the saucepan. Bring it back to the boil and remove from heat and stir in the agar agar (or gelatine) and make sure it is well dissolved. Allow to cool.

6. Place the drained rhubarb and strawberries into a serving bowl and cover with the jelly syrup. Place on a level shelf in the fridge and chill until the jelly is set.

7. Serve with a scoop of the crème fraiche or frozen yoghurt and a sugar-free chocolate biscuit.

The fruit in this jelly is high fibre and naturally sweet.
Set in a glass for alternative presentation.

one ounce one carb exchange equals 15grams or half an ounce

2

Hot sweet citrus & almond bake

SERVES 4

juice and zest of 3 lemons or
limes

3 fl oz milk (2% fat)

3 egg yolks

4 egg whites

¼ teaspoon vanilla bean paste
or essence

6oz (150g) ground almonds

3 tablespoons self-raising/bakers
flour

2 tablespoons milk powder

1 tablespoon caster/superfine
sugar

1 tablespoon slivered almonds

butter for greasing

4fl oz (120ml) light cream
sweetened with a little agave

1. Preheat oven to 360°F/180°C. Prepare a bain marie hot water bath.

2. Zest the lemons into a bowl with the lemon juice (approx 4 fl oz 120ml). Add the egg yolks, agave nectar and vanilla paste.

3. Mix together the almonds and the flour. Mix them into the egg yolk and lemon mixture and combine the milk.

4. In another bowl whisk the egg whites to stiff peaks, add the caster sugar, then fold these whites into the mixture carefully, do not over mix.

5. Lightly grease a baking dish or ovenproof glass bowl and pour the mixture in. Sprinkle the top with slithered almonds.

6. Bake immediately in the bain marie hot water bath in the oven for 20 minutes.

7. Serve with a little sweetened cream.

A twist on the classic lemon delicious for the middle of the table, in winter or summer.

Toffee, carrot, honey & nut slice

MAKES 1 LARGE TRAY, APPROXIMATELY 12 SERVES

12oz (350g) fresh full cream
  ricotta cheese
2 tablespoons agave nectar
4 fl oz (120ml) fresh milk (2% fat)
2oz (60g) butter
1 tablespoon vegetable oil
6oz (175g) self-raising/bakers
  flour
½ teaspoon bicarbonate of soda
2oz (60g) ground almonds
3 large fresh eggs
6oz (175g) fresh carrot, grated
2oz (60g) walnuts, roughly
  chopped
2 oz (60g) slithered almonds
2oz (60g) pistachio nuts,
  chopped
4oz (120g) crème fraiche for
  frosting, sweetened with a little
  agave nectar
Icing sugar or cinnamon to dust

1. Preheat oven to 360°F/180°C. Using an electric mixer, beat the ricotta for 3 minutes on a high speed until very smooth.

2. In a small saucepan melt the agave nectar with the milk, butter and oil then allow to cool.

3. In a bowl, sift together the flour, bicarbonate of soda and the ground almonds.

4. Reduce the mixer speed to slow, then gradually add the eggs and the milk mixture. Add the ground almonds and flour and combine together, but do not over mix.

5. Add the grated carrots and the chopped walnuts, slithered almonds and the pistachio nuts. Stir and mix through.

6. Grease and line a large toffee tray with baking parchment and spread the mixture evenly into it. Bake in oven for 30 minutes until firm to touch, remove from the oven and allow to cool in the tray. Using a large knife score the cake into portions approximately 2inches/5cm square or to your liking. Spread some crème fraiche on the top or dust with cinnamon or a little icing sugar.

191

Citrus & Poppy Seed Cake

SERVES 12

CAKE MIXTURE

2 lemons

3 large oranges

3 cups of water

3 tablespoons agave nectar

2 cardamom pods

1oz (30g) butter

3 eggs lightly beaten

8oz (240g) ground almonds

2 tablespoons poppy seeds

2 tablespoons self-raising/bakers
 flour

2 tablespoons whey protein
 powder

1 teaspoon bicarbonate of soda

SYRUP

2 tablespoons freshly squeezed
 orange juice

juice of ¼ of a lemon

1 tablespoon agave nectar

1. Peel lemons and oranges, discard rind, and slice fruit approximately ¼inch/5mm thick.

2. Place fruit in a medium sized saucepan with the water, agave nectar and 2 cardamom pods. Cover with a lid and place on a medium heat to simmer for approximately 2 hours until the fruit is totally cooked and broken down, and has a marmalade-like consistency. Take care not to burn as it will become very sticky as it nears the end of its cooking.

3. Preheat oven to 360°F/180°C.

4. Remove the cardamom pods and discard. Stir in the butter to melt and allow mixture to cool.

5. Place fruit into a mixing bowl and mix in the lightly beaten eggs.

6. Stir in the ground almonds, protein powder, bicarbonate of soda, poppy seeds and the flour. Mix well together. It will be quite loose at this point.

7. Line an 8inch/20cm cake tin with greaseproof paper and a spray of oil. Pour in the cake mixture and bake for 25 minutes until golden and firm to touch.

8. Meanwhile, to make the syrup, warm the lemon and orange juice with the agave.

9. Once cooked, remove the cake from the oven and allow to cool on a cooling wire. Turn it over and place onto your serving plate, brush it with the warm syrup and allow it to soak in.

cinnamon apple upside-down pudding

SERVES 4

4 red apples
2oz (60g) butter
1 teaspoon ground cinnamon
pinch ground cloves
pinch ground nutmeg
3 tablespoons agave nectar

PUDDING MIXTURE
4oz (120g) fresh ricotta
½ teaspoon vanilla essence
4 fl oz (120ml) milk (2% fat)
2oz (60g) butter
2 eggs, separated
1 teaspoon caster/superfine
   sugar
2 tablespoons ground almonds
2 tablespoons self-raising/bakers
   flour, sifted
2 tablespoons flaked almonds

1. Preheat oven to 320°F/160°C. Peel, core and cut each apple into 8 wedges.

2. Melt 2oz (60g) butter in a small pan with the spices and 2 tablespoons agave nectar. Coat the apple wedges in this and place wedges onto a non-stick baking tray. Bake in oven for 20 minutes until soft and caramelised.

3. Remove from the oven and while still hot place apple wedges into a deep ovenproof baking dish (I like to use a glass dish for this).

4. Warm the milk and vanilla with the remaining 1 tablespoon of agave nectar and 2 oz (60g) of butter, melt together and then allow it to cool.

5. In a mixer beat the ricotta for 3 minutes until smooth and creamy, add the egg yolks and the milk mxture. Then mix in the ground almonds and flour combine together.

6. In a separate bowl, whisk the egg whites to a stiff peak with the caster sugar. Fold these egg whites into the mixture and pour mixture over the caramalised apples, sprinkle the top with the flaked almonds.

7. Bake in the oven for 30 minutes until golden and firm to the touch.

Serve this warm as a great alternative to apple pie, without the fat or sugar content.

Basics

Pickled sweet chilies

MAKES APPROXIMATELY 6 SERVES

½ teaspoon yellow mustard
   seeds
1 cup of water
3 tablespoons of red wine
   vinegar
1 small onion, finely sliced
1 slice of lemon
1 tablespoon of caster/superfine
   sugar
pinch sea salt
8 medium-sized red chilies, finely
   sliced
1 tablespoon agave nectar
1 tablespoon olive oil

1. Heat a small saucepan over a low heat and toast mustard seeds for 1 minute. Pour in the water, add the red wine vinegar, onion and lemon slice. Bring to the boil and stir in the caster sugar and the salt.

2. Add the sliced chilies and bring back to the boil. Remove from the heat immediately. Allow to cool in the saucepan.

3. Once cool, remove the lemon and drain well. Place chilies into a small bowl, stir through the agave nectar and a tablespoon of olive oil.

I enjoy these chilies so much more than the commercial sweet chili sauce. Use wherever chilies are called, for example beef ribs or sliders. These are a staple in my fridge.

TOMATO KETCHUP

MAKES ONE LARGE JAR

12oz (350g) can crushed
   tomatoes
1 tablespoon tomato paste
1 tablespoon agave nectar
1 teaspoon dried onion flakes
½ clove garlic, crushed
Small pinch ground cinnamon
Small pinch ground cloves
pinch sweet paprika
2 tablespoons malt vinegar
1oz (30g)cornflour, mixed with 1
   tablespoon of cold water

1. In a medium-sized saucepan bring all ingredients, except the cornflour, mixture to the boil for 1 minute.

2. Stir in the cornflour mixture, whisk and cook for 30 seconds or until it thickens.

3. Using a stick blender, puree the sauce and pass through a fine strainer. Allow to cool before pouring into a jar. This will keep in the fridge for 2 weeks.

There is so much sugar in commercial ketchup, this is a great alternative sauce.

MY steak sauce

MAKES APPROXIMATELY 4 SERVES

4 tablespoon tomato ketchup
   sauce (see Basics section)
1 teaspoon English mustard
½ bunch tarragon leaves
   chopped
1 teaspoon Worcestershire Sauce
pinch dried chili flakes

1. Simply mix together, store in the fridge and serve when required.

Ideal for fish, meat or grilled vegetables.

Low-fat, whole egg mayonnaise

MAKES APPROXIMATELY 2 CUPS

1 large fresh egg
2 egg whites
1 tablespoon protein powder
juice of half a lemon
1 teaspoon Dijon mustard
6 fl oz (175ml) light canola oil
1 tablespoon chardonnay or
  white wine vinegar
4oz (120g) natural Greek
  yoghurt
pinch sea salt and fresh black
  pepper
pinch cayenne pepper

1. In a large mixing bowl, use a large whisk to whisk the egg, egg whites, vinegar and protein powder together with the lemon juice and mustard.

2. Drizzle in the oil in, taking care to combine it each time before adding more. Once all combined and emulsified, whisk in the yoghurt and season with salt, pepper and a pinch of cayenne pepper.

A great base for sandwich fillings or other creamy style dressings and even simply as a vegetable dip.

Asian Vinaigrette

MAKES 1 MEDIUM-SIZED JAR

½ fresh fennel bulb

juice and zest of 2 limes

2 tablespoons dark soy sauce

4 tablespoons canola oil

1 tablespoon white sesame
  seeds, lightly toasted

½ bunch fresh coriander/cilantro
  leaves

1 teaspoon fermented chili bean
  paste

1 clove garlic

½ teaspoon fish sauce

1. Place all ingredients into a medium sized jar with a screw lid.
2. Seal tightly and shake well.

vegetable stock

MAKES 2 PINTS (1L)

1 head of fennel, shredded
1 medium onion, shredded
2½ pints (1¼ L) water
1 medium sized carrot
1 tablespoon of coriander/
    cilantro seeds
1 teaspoon fennel seeds
1 teaspoon black peppercorns
2 fresh bay leaves
1 bunch parsley
pinch of sea salt

1. In a small saucepan, place the chopped fennel and onion, pour in enough water to cover, then bring to the boil. Drain and refresh under cold water to remove any bitterness.

2. In a medium-sized pan place fennel and onions with all remaining ingredients and cover with water. Bring quickly to the boil and hold at a rolling simmer for 5 minutes.

3. Remove from the heat and cool in an ice bath or in the fridge.

Tip: If this stock is to be used same day strain out all vegetables and use as required. Alternatively strain and freeze using an ice cube tray.

Fresh and light and a great base for almost all hot soups or sauces.

Low-fat Cheese & Chipotle Sauce

MAKES 6 SERVES

625ml (20fl oz) low-fat milk
1 small dried bay leaf
1 tablespoon low-fat spread/
   margarine
1 tablespoon plain (all-purpose)
   flour
1 teaspoon Dijon mustard
2 tablespoons low-fat cheddar
   cheese, grated
2 tablespoons parmesan cheese,
   grated
½ teaspoon chipotle chili
freshly ground white pepper

1. Warm milk and bay leaf together until hot. Remove bay leaf and set aside.

2. Melt spread in medium saucepan and stir in flour to form a paste (roux). Cook for 2 minutes. Gradually stir in a third of the milk and cook until it comes to the boil and thickens.

3. Gradually add the rest of the milk and continue to cook until sauce comes to the boil and thickens. Whisk out any lumps.

4. Slowly simmer, covered with a lid, for 4 to 5 minutes. Remove from the heat. Add mustard and cheeses and chipotle and stir until melted. Season to taste with white pepper.

Lemon, lime & orange vinaigrette

MAKES 6 SERVES

juice of 1 lemon
juice of 1 lime
juice of ½ orange
1 teaspoon seeded mustard
1 teaspoon Dijon mustard
½ teaspoon agave nectar
60ml (2fl oz) extra virgin olive oil
pinch of sea salt and freshly
   ground black pepper

1. Whisk ingredients together and season to taste with salt and pepper. Alternatively, place into a screw top jar and shake just before using.

2. Refrigerate until required for up to two weeks.

The Family
Kitchen

"You will always win on flavor if you make it yourself."

"A small amount of something good is better than a large amount of poor quality."

MY 5 White Devils
MY 5 Tasty Angels

I constantly try to focus my diet on taste and healthy eating. To make it easier for me, I know I have to avoid my 5 White Devils. I keep them in my mind at all times. They are foods that I try to eliminate or at least reduce to a bare minimum. If you do the same, I am sure you will feel better and healthier and you may even shed a few kilos as a bonus.

All the devils have a hi Gi, so the carbohydrate is converted or broken down into glucose in our bodies very quickly and with almost immediate effect. This causes a spike in blood sugar levels.

For me this requires increased amounts of insulin or to do some physical exercise.

My 5 Angels are the food alternatives that are far better for your body. These too are always in my mind.

After a while, a swap between Devils and Angels becomes an automatic reflex.

215

MY 5 WHITE DEVILS

1. WHITE RICE

I used to love to eat white rice. There are about 40,000 varieties of rice, it is cheap and easy to grow and is the staple food for a large part of the world's population. For people with diabetes white rice and its derived products need to go. This includes rice crackers and rice noodles, as well as sticky coconut rice desserts. There are some smart, low Gi rice varieties available, but in my opinion they are the best of a bad bunch.

2. WHITE FLOUR

It is time to remove white flour from your diet. This includes all white bread, cakes, muffins and biscuits that are made with highly processed white flour, as well as fat and sugar. I really don't miss white bread and for me this has been the easiest Devil to remove from my meal choices. Cheese biscuits are also off the menu.

I try to select products that have been made with wholegrain flour or contain high levels of nuts, seeds or grains. If you must have white bread, choose the more artisan style of handmade sourdough bread.

Some people think that Turkish bread is healthy, but it also has high Gi.

If you choose wraps, try to pick wholegrain flour wraps. One advantage with wraps is the low volume you eat. Try to fill them with lean protein and vegetables.

The flour used in pizza making is often the same as white bread. Pizza can be covered in high fat cheese toppings. Always choose a thin crust pizza and add lean protein and fresh vegetables as much as possible.

3. WHITE PASTA

There is some debate about pasta and how much you should eat and whether it should be classed as a Devil. For me it is dangerous because it can be hi Gi but also it is a high volume product. I tend to eat far more for a portion size and always feel so full after eating it. So I have chosen to call it one of My White Devils.

Some pasta has a lower Gi, so if you must eat it try to choose the artisan bronze extruded pasta made from durum wheat (it has a matte look to it).

The real problem comes from the sauces you add. Try to use less sauce and focus on lean meats, seafood and vegetables. Learn to make a nice tomato base sauce rather than cheese or cream based sauces. Good pasta will hold more sauce and taste delicious.

4. WHITE POTATOES

We all love potatoes. They vary in Gi and there are many varieties but they are all high in carbohydrate.

I try to have a zero policy for myself when it comes to potatoes, because once I start I have little will power to stop. Who doesn't like crispy roasted potatoes or crunchy potato chips? These are often served laden with salt and they are highly absorbent when cooked in fat. The variety to look out for are Nicola or Charisma, as they are good eating and have the lowest Gi of all potatoes.

5. WHITE SUGAR

As a person with diabetes I am not allergic to sugar. In fact, normal table sugar has a moderate Gi and is far from the worst thing I could eat. It can be a good help in reversing any low sugar hypo that I have. For someone living with diabetes, their bodies break down sugars into glucose in exactly the same way, but their bodies cannot absorb it as effectively which can cause a build up of glucose in the blood.

Try your best to remove white sugar from your diet and try to reduce any type of sugar. It is hidden everywhere in processed products. Cordial, jams and soft drinks also have high sugar levels.

MY 5 TASTY ANGELS

1. QUINOA, BUCKWHEAT AND BARLEY

Replace white rice and pasta in your pantry with these and learn how to cook them. They have a lower Gi and taste fantastic. They can also help to bulk out a meal for someone who is really hungry.

2. SEEDED WHOLEGRAIN BREAD AND SOURDOUGH

Let's face it we all love bread. The less processed, the better it is for us and wholegrain is the buzzword.

Soy and linseed (flax seed) bread is my favorite.

A handmade artisan sourdough loaf to me is a thing of beauty and as a bonus it is on the good side of the spectrum just eat in moderation.

3. BEANS, CHICKPEAS AND LENTILS

I love these ingredients I use them in salads or in meat stews and braises, they help to bulk a dish and add some protein to it. As for pasta, be careful with the sauces you make try to focus on tomato based ones rather than cream or cheese.

4. SWEET POTATOES

I try to replace white potatoes with delicious, orange sweet potatoes whenever I can. I've grown to enjoy their flavor more and more. They have many nutrients and minerals in them and they have a moderate Gi. They can be cooked in the same way as white potatoes. Try them and see.

5. AGAVE NECTAR AND SWEETNERS

It should be said that agave nectar and syrup is still sugar, but as it is sweeter than sugar, you need less of it. It is my sugar swap of choice. I prefer its flavor and use it in many of my recipes. It is great to cook with. There are many sugar alternatives on the market, I try to encourage people to reduce their intake of artificial sweeteners if they can.

Replace white
flour bread with
wholemeal, seeded
or artisan bread.

Replace white
rice with quinoa,
seeds, buckwheat
or barley.

Replace white
potatoes with
sweet potatoes.

Replace white
pasta with
beans, chickpeas
and lentils.

The Family Pantry

Let's take a look inside your pantry.

• Sugars

I urge you to remove as many refined sugars from your pantry as possible. These include cordials ,jams and syrups. Pure honey and maple syrup have a lower Gi than processed sugars, but need to be consumed in moderation. I replace jams with some mashed fresh strawberries or raspberries with a little agave nectar. I spread this on toast which has far less impact on my blood sugars than normal jams or even fruit spreads.

• Spices

Try to increase your consumption of dried spices, especially chili, as these ingredients can stimulate your metabolism while improving the flavor of your dish. Dried herbs are convenient, however they lack the antioxidants of fresh herbs. Personally I love fresh herbs and use plenty of them in my cooking.

• Tea and coffee

I love good coffee! There has recently been some evidence to show that a small amount of espresso coffee can help reduce diabetes. Herbal teas are delicious and can help hydrate you. Why not swap dried teas and learn to make fresh herb teas? Fresh garden mint and lemon are among my favorites.

• Sweet biscuits, nut bars and cakes

I was born with a sweet tooth and really enjoy a cup of tea with a sweet biscuit, so I have had to train myself to resist these things. The best thing to do is not to buy them—do not have them in your house and you will not be so tempted in a moment of weakness. I have included a great recipe for slices in this book as they are really easy to make and you can swap the nuts and seeds to your own taste. Kids love to eat things they have made. If you learn to make cakes rather than buy them, you will have more control over the ingredients.

• Canned food

No one would expect a chef to recommend that you use or buy canned food, but in reality they can save time and help make a meal healthier. Canned tuna and salmon in spring water are great sources of protein and are readily available—try to select low salt options.

    I always suggest washing dried chickpeas, lentils or beans before I use them.

One of my favorite snacks is sardines on toast—they have good protein and fish oils as well as calcium content from the fish bones. A salmon and tuna three bean salad with some fresh herbs is a great fast food and can be mostly made from canned products.

• Dried goods

When you clean out all of the white rice and reduce the pasta in your pantry, you will have room for buckwheat, barley and my favorite, quinoa. This is available in white, red or black. Quinoa is easy to cook and is really tasty. It also gives you a feeling of fullness without the feeling of being bloated or over indulged.

• Breakfast cereals

If you have children, they usually will want sweetened cereals. If you read the labels you will see amazing high levels of sugar, and add this to the fact that they are highly processed and you have a double whammy. They should be avoided full stop. Even cereals with bran flakes have a high Gi because of the processing method.

Try to buy some unprocessed bran to add to your breakfast—fresh berries with a little natural yoghurt and some bran is delicious and good for you.

If you like to eat porridge, try to cook traditional rolled oats or steel-cut oats, not the quick one minute packs or pre mixed and sweetened oats. I always mix in some rolled barley oats or quinoa—these have a lower Gi and taste great.

• Sauces and marinades

There is so much sugar and salt hidden in processed sauces. Try to limit your use of them or experiment and make some fresh sauces—they may not keep as long but they will taste so much better. Soy sauce and Asian teriyaki sauces and marinades are often full of salt and sugar. Try to limit your consumption of these. Instead, use fresh chili, herbs, lemon and garlic or dried pepper spice mixes as a healthy choice.

• Oil and vinegar

Don't be fooled by the labelling. 'Light olive oil' is light in flavor but not fat—it is over 90% fat. Often light oil is produced by chemical extraction.

I recommend a high quality extra virgin oil as the best option. Swap butter for extra virgin olive oil in your cooking where possible. This oil is high in monounsaturated fats and antioxidants where as butter is high in saturated fat and bad for your cholesterol levels.

Be careful with thick or flavored vinegars or glazes they are usually full of sugar. Caramelised balsamic vinegar can be as high as 60% sugar. Good quality vinegar can make the difference between a good and a bad salad.

The Family Fridge and Freezer

I think the fridge is the hub of every home—it certainly is in mine and it's usually covered in photos and reminders of upcoming sports events and notes. The fridge is also the first place most of us go when looking for a snack.

The key to helping reduce temptation is the same as the pantry—if you don't buy it in the first place it simply won't be there.

The freezer can be a great help in planning meals and can assist you to eat well. I cook in large batches, especially soups and braises, sauces and baked dishes, and freeze the extra amounts.

Lurking in the freezer is one of my great weaknesses—ice cream and sorbet. It is a slippery slope for me. My wife has discovered some low sugar and low-fat products and unfortunately they do not taste as good as the real thing, but it's all that I am allowed! I have created a simple semi freddo recipe in this book as a replacement and I love frozen yoghurt. I am always trying new homemade flavors sweetened with a little fresh fruit, vanilla or agave nectar.

• Dairy products

We all need some Vitamin D in our bodies and dairy products are rich in that. I still try to eat low-fat dairy or only a very small amount of full cream dairy products. In the US, 2% milk is a great all round milk. I notice on my travels it is becoming popular everywhere.

If you don't have a sweet tooth then it's likely that you love cheese. If this is you, try to enjoy the harder cheeses and keep away from the creamy brie and soft style cheeses. Hard cheeses have less fat and we tend to eat less of them as well.

• Yoghurt

This can be the most confusing product for people who are new to reading labels and watching their diet. The marketing of yoghurt has been so successful for so long that we tend to believe that all yoghurt is good for you.

Natural yoghurt in its simplest form is a great product to cook with. I use it in desserts and starters as well as dressings and drinks. It can still have up to 8% sugar and is a carbohydrate, however it can also have some great cultures and healthy bacteria that is good for you. Rather than preach to you I suggest you read some labels and find the yoghurt you like and one that is available. Beware of low-fat flavored ones as the labels often forget to mention the sugar level.

Some frozen yoghurt is often sold as an alternative to ice cream. Always check the sugar level before eating it.

• Butter

In my training as a chef I would use a lot of butter, now I tend to be more careful with it. I do still like to use good quality butter but I reduce the amount to the absolute minimum.

There are plenty of other spreads on the market—olive oil spreads and margarine promise a wide range of benefits. I suggest you find the one you like the best and eat as little of it as possible, then enjoy a small amount of good butter on special occasions.

• Eggs

Eggs are a super food in my fridge. The whites are a fantastic source of protein and as a whole they create many great meal options. I buy only fresh free range eggs where possible—they cost a little more but you can really taste the difference.

• Meat and fresh fish

The key to shopping for fresh meat and fish is to buy just what you need and if possible get to know the person you are buying it from.

Lean meat is a great base for a healthy meal and if possible should be a part of most meals you eat. Protein is broken down more slowly by the body, so it can have the overall effect of reducing the total Gi of your meals.

Protein is also good for muscle growth. This is also a benefit as a muscular body performs better.

Salmon is a great 'go to' fish for me, mostly because it is readily available all over the world. It also freezes very well. I like salmon both raw and cooked. It is high in good fish oils and relatively cheap to buy. I always try to eat sustainable seafood and would encourage everyone else to as well.

As far as beef is concerned, I try only to eat lean grass-fed meat. It is higher in Omegas and for me has a superior flavor. Grain fed meat has higher saturated fat levels (saturated fats are found in animal-derived products).

You will find plenty of advice on how you should cook meat. I prefer to simply grill it.

Chickens are also a great source of protein—the skin holds a lot of the fat but a nicely poached chicken breast is a great healthy part of a meal or sandwich. I try to buy as best quality as possible and free range or organic are my choice.

People with diabetes should avoid too much sweet corn, however it is fine for us to eat corn-fed chickens. They can be delicious and have the same protein and Gi as regular chickens.

Extreme Vegetable Shopping

I love shopping for fresh vegetables and fruit. It connects me with the season and inspires me to get cooking.

I urge you to change your mindset in line with mine and go to fresh food markets as often as possible. Don't be shy to buy a whole tray of something in season and in ripe condition. You will notice how cheap it is and you will be able to create a few different dishes, maybe even freeze them for later.

Each vegetable has its own character but my recommendation is just to eat what you enjoy, the benefits of eating fresh vegetables far outweigh any side effects. My only advice would be to limit the starchy ones like tarot, potatoes, some yams and pumpkins (due to the higher Gi as mentioned before.)

Some sweet vegetables like corn and carrots should be eaten in moderation, but for the rest I say go for it!

Salads! I really love a fresh salad. It is easy to turn a salad into a healthy main course and feed a large group, they always look great and create a wonderful casual sharing meal. Ripeness and season is the key to good flavor.

Eating Out In Restaurants

Every now and again we all like to go to restaurants and as a restaurateur I encourage you all to do so as often as possible. For me, whatever the type of restaurant you choose, you should be able to navigate your way through the menu and eat well. All cuisines have a simple variation on grilled meat or fish and salad or vegetables. Try to avoid heavily fried food or processed food, you will feel better for it in the morning.

Thai food can be full of palm sugar and coconut milk or cream. Try to eat the protein and vegetables from the curry rather than all of the sauce. Asian or fast food can be full of salt, fat and high in carbohydrate, so try to avoid it as much as possible and only ever eat a small amount of rice with it.

Moderation is the key. I want to encourage everyone to have a healthy but fun life, full of the joy that great food and sharing can bring.

Exercise

If you have a sedentary lifestyle then I suggest firstly that you move more. Try to get as active as possible, which is good for your brain and mood as much as it is for your body. If you have become overweight and find it hard to get motivated, I would suggest swimming, walking and light running is the best exercise to start with.

My personal trainer Dan Dierke has generously contributed four points that he recommends that we try to follow:

1. INCREASE YOUR AMOUNT OF INCIDENTAL EXERCISE—JUST MOVE
It couldn't be made clearer or any easier. The more active you are the healthier you become. Take the stairs, ditch the elevator and walk whenever you can. Leave your car in the garage.

2. RESISTANCE TRAINING (WEIGHT TRAINING)
This could be the single most important aspect of any exercise regime and possibly second only to nutrition. This is essential for improved bone density, body posture and injury prevention. Push ups are a great way to get started.

3. INTENSITY AND FREQUENCY
I am always asked how much and how hard. Just start! At first walk every day with a family member before work or school. Just 30 minutes a day is enough to have a benefit. Then gradually increase your distance or start jogging intervals during your walk.

4. SCHEDULING YOUR WEEK
Plan ahead in your diary time to exercise. If your phone is you closest companion set a series of reminders.

EXAMPLES:
Here are some examples that you can use in your new weekly training plan. Almost every activity mentioned can and should be done by the entire family. Stay hydrated during this activity. Here are some ideas: football, frisbee, kicking any type of ball, tennis, squash, cycling, bush walking, indoor rock climbing, swimming, surfing, rollerblading, cricket.

ABOUT THE AUTHOR

Michael Moore is an experienced and respected chef, starting out in some of London's best restaurants. Now 26 years into a career spanning two continents, Michael has owned and managed numerous top restaurants in both London and Sydney including The Ritz Hotel London, Kables, Craigend, Hotel Nikko, The Bluebird London, Bennelong, Prunier's, Bonne Femme and Wildfire. Michael has earned critical appraise on both sides of the globe, as well as a number of coveted media awards. Michael has appeared on television for the last seven years and is currently the chef and owner of O Bar and Dining in Sydney. *Blood Sugar: The Family* is Michael's third book, and follows *Moore to Food* and *Blood Sugar*.

www.michaelmoorechef.com
www.obardining.com.au
twitter: @michaelmooresyd

facebook: \chefmichaelmoore

Weights and Measures

½ metric teaspoon	2.5ml
1 metric teaspoon	5ml
2 teaspoons	10ml
1 tablespoon	20ml

CUPS

All measures are based on level cupfuls.

LIQUID

1 cup	250ml (9fl oz)
½ cup	125ml (4fl oz)

SOLIDS

1 cup flour	120g (4oz)
1 cup white sugar	180g (6oz)
1 cup light brown sugar	120g (4oz)
1 cup caster sugar	120g (4oz)
1 cup chopped nuts	180g (6oz)
1 cup grated cheese	90g (3oz)

OVEN TEMPERATURES

100°C	very slow	200°F	Gas Mark 1
120°C	very slow	250°F	Gas Mark 1
150°C	slow	300°F	Gas Mark 2
160°C	warm	325°F	Gas Mark 2–3
180°C	moderate	350°F	Gas Mark 4
190°C	moderately hot	375°F	Gas Mark 5
200°C	moderately hot	400°F	Gas Mark 6
220°C	hot	420°F	Gas Mark 7
230°C	very hot	450°F	Gas Mark 8
250°C	very hot	485°F	Gas Mark 9

ACKNOWLEDGEMENTS

Wow what a journey I am on. My life has been enriched by my family and friends, all of whom give me unconditional love and support. My truly amazing wife Angela and my extended family, my delightful inspiring children Charlie and Eloise, my mother Lesley, sister Lisa, Dad and my mother-in-law Kay—all have contributed to make me the person I have become. Thank you—my endless love and commitment is yours.

In my professional life many people have worked for me and I would like to recognize and thank them all for their hard work. My current team are the best ever and have helped give birth to this book and launch my restaurant O Bar and Dining. What a year! It's been amazing.

There is one person who has worked so tirelessly for me and has become integral to my success and happiness—he has almost become family. Steven McArthur you really are one in a million—thank you.

Fiona and Lliane from New Holland—you have done it again and your never-ending support has helped me to produce a beautiful cookbook. You are just the best in the game.

Steve Brown is just the easiest to work with and the most humble, talented food photographer in Australia—thanks mate. Thanks to Babette Perry, Lisa Mitchell and the IMG team for their support and commitment to help me achieve my potential.

This year has seen me become a contributing member of the diabetec community on a global scale, hopefully inspiring people to find joy and make the best of their situation. Simon Scott and the team at Sanofi Australia, thank you. I believe we can move mountains together and that the iBGStar can change lives.

Most of all I would like to acknowledge all the people living with diabetes, and their carers, who have shared their stories and challenges with me. They have pushed me to create this book.

First published in 2013 by New Holland Publishers Pty Ltd   London • Sydney • Cape Town • Auckland

Garfield House 86–88 Edgware Road London W2 2EA United Kingdom; 1/66 Gibbes Street Chatswood NSW 2067 Australia
218 Lake Road Northcote Auckland New Zealand; Wembley Square First Floor Solan Road Gardens Cape Town 8001 South Africa

www.newhollandpublishers.com; www.newholland.com.au

A record of this book is held at the National Library of Australia   ISBN 9781742573090

Publisher: Fiona Schultz
Publishing director: Lliane Clarke
Designer: Tracy Loughlin
Proofreader: Catherine Etteridge
Photographs: Steve Brown Photography
Props and styling assistance: Yael Grinham
Production director: Olga Dementiev
Printer: Toppan Leefung (China) Ltd

10 9 8 7 6 5 4 3 2 1

Keep up with New Holland Publishers on Facebook   http://www.facebook.com/NewHollandPublishers
Twitter: @NewHollandAU

Our thanks to Harris Farm Markets and The Grounds Alexandria for permission to use their locations.

Index of recipes

This edition published by Parragon Books Ltd in 2015

Parragon Books Ltd
Chartist House
15–17 Trim Street
Bath BA1 1HA, UK
www.parragon.com

ISBN 978-1-4748-1656-4

Printed in China